The BOTTOM LINE is Betrayal

Third Edition

Katherine T. Smith

with
L. Murphy Smith
Texas A&M University
and
D. Larry Crumbley
Louisiana State University

2000

DAME
PUBLICATIONS, INC.

Cover Design: Andrea P. Leggett

7800 Bissonnet–Suite 415
Houston, TX 77074
(800) 364-9757
(713) 995-1000
(713) 995-9637–FAX
E-mail: dame.publications@worldnet.att.net
Website: http://www.damepub.com

ISBN 0-87393-886-0

Library of Congress Card No. 97-67097

Printed in the United States of America.

THE BOTTOM LINE IS BETRAYAL

For the Instructor

The Bottom Line is Betrayal is a fictional business novel which delves into the operation of a multinational corporation and whose characters demonstrate practical applications of business concepts. The novel will help your students understand and relate to the subject you're teaching. The characters use the skills of business and technology to solve problems such as increasing sales, improving accounting procedures, safeguarding computer information, and analyzing the international market and general economy.

Using the novel in your class is easy: simply make it a reading assignment and ask students for a book report. If you want to do more, test questions and a team project are provided in appendices at the end of the book. *The Bottom Line is Betrayal* is designed for use in any business course, specifically to supplement coverage of information technology and international trade issues. It is especially well suited for an Introduction to Business class because it demonstrates how diverse business fields, accounting, economics, finance, management, and marketing, work together for the overall success of the firm.

Mystery and intrigue are synonymous with the novel's protagonist, Moses McDonald, a professor and business consultant who has been hired by Coca-Cola. While on the job, Moses and his assistant, Duke, uncover a scheme that could jeopardize Coke's future existence. Fraud, corporate espionage, international politics, and devastating betrayal place Moses and his colleagues in life-threatening situations. They must travel overseas and use state-of-the-art technology to solve the problem. So pull on your trench coat, put on your fedora, and enjoy a good, educational read.

DEDICATION

To Mom and Dad

ACKNOWLEDGMENT

The author acknowledges her collaborators, D. Larry Crumbley, L. Murphy Smith, and Hugh Nations, whose earlier work concerning auditing contributed to the storyline. Additionally, the author appreciates the helpful comments, suggestions, and encouragement provided by Charles Alworth, Dalene Barnes, John E. Delaney, Art Francia, Cliff Francis, Sharon Hurley Johns, Michael Licata, Stephen W. McDaniel, Bill McDowell, John W. Meredith, Jeff Miller, Steve McDuffie, Douglas W. Mellott, Jr., Judy Moore, Barbara Morris, Grover Porter, Bill Pride, Lawrence C. Smith, Jr., Carolyn Strand, Carol Sullivan, and Hal Teer.

WEBSITE

http://www.IOL19.com/murphy/novels/novels.htm

THE BOTTOM LINE IS BETRAYAL

TABLE OF CONTENTS

THE BOTTOM LINE IS BETRAYAL

Chapter 1

Man is the only animal who drinks when he isn't thirsty.
Mark Twain

Moses McDonald could feel the grip of the nagging tension relaxing its hold just the slightest as he drank his Cherry Coke. It brought back boyhood memories. The flavor was slightly reminiscent of the Cherry Cokes he used to drink at the soda fountain of his old neighborhood drugstore. He then thought about his new consulting job. He was rather pleased that the Coca Cola Company had hired him. After all, Coke was a major international business firm. It was one of the 30 companies included in the Dow Jones Industrial Average, the stock market barometer. The thought of being paid by the company that manufactured his beverage made each sip particularly refreshing.

He and his daughter were now residing in Atlanta, the queen city of the South. As he thought about his new home, Moses began recalling scenes from the epic motion picture, *Gone With The Wind.* Moses had a passion for history and had read numerous books about the Civil War. As wars go, it was an exceptionally tragic one. Families were divided by the conflict. Even President and Mrs. Lincoln had family members fighting on each side. The city of Atlanta was burned to the ground by the Union forces under General William Tecumseh Sherman. For many years, people with the surname of Sherman felt a little uncomfortable passing through Georgia.

Moses looked at his daughter and mused with a twinge of regret. Katie soon would be partaking of all the joys of adulthood -- independence, self-reliance, marriage, children; not to mention, mortgages, traffic jams, income taxes, and the daily grind. Katie strongly resembled his late wife. His wife hadn't been beautiful, but he had counted himself lucky to win her over the many suitors who, like himself, had been attracted by her enthusiasm for life. Watching Katie as she had walked away to the ladies' room, Moses thought about his daughter's next 10 or 12 years. He reflected how adolescence, college, and establishing a career had been some of the most adventuresome times of his life. He suspected Katie would fit right into the Southern ambiance, despite her initial reluctance at leaving Philadelphia.

Just now, Moses himself was feeling a trifle uncomfortable, and after a moment he finally was able to identify the source. It was the atmosphere in the lobby bar at the Peachtree Plaza. Well ... not the atmosphere so much as the surroundings.

The lobby bar was one of the city's showcases; the tables were virtually islands set in an indoor lagoon. All that water had brought to mind Moses' terrible experience on the Paddlewheel Pancake House, a riverboat restaurant specializing in breakfast foods. He worked as a waiter on the boat during the summer between his junior and senior year of college. Like most small businesses, the riverboat restaurant went under after a short time. The owner failed to do any market research to determine whether there would be enough customers. The worst part of working there wasn't the low pay or lousy tips. The worst part was the night he fell overboard.

The unfortunate incident occurred on the night that Sigma Alpha Pi, a social sorority, chartered the boat for a four-hour evening cruise, pancake dinner, and dance. He had only been working a week and was just getting accustomed to the boat. While walking rapidly with a large tray of pigs-in-a-blanket held over his shoulder and making serious eye contact with a sorority member, he failed to notice where some water had been spilt on the deck. Moses' feet slipped, and while balancing his tray of food, he slid four feet into a waist-high guard rail. He came to an abrupt stop on impact with the rail but inertia kept the tray going. In his efforts to regain control of the hors d'oeuvres, he fell over the rail and into the river.

The Peachtree Plaza was an extravagant edifice -- the tallest hotel in the nation, and the view from the Sun Dial, the revolving bar atop the 74-story hotel, was without parallel in the city. Katie and he had visited the Sun Dial briefly last night, just long enough for each to have a soft drink. Moses had been even more uneasy then, and it had nothing to do with water. He just didn't like being stuck that high up, with no way to get down in the event of a fire.

Moses had to admit, however, that the view from the bar was worth the visit. Patrons could follow the course of world-famed Peachtree Street as it wound northward for miles through the city toward the affluent Sandy Springs and Roswell area. Looking out on the panorama, Moses had even been able to point out the imposing granite bulk of Stone Mountain to the east.

Just as the Peachtree Plaza was an architectural extravagance, Moses thought that this stay was an extravagance for him as well. On earlier visits, he had chosen more modest accommodations. This time Katie would get her first impression of her new home, and Moses wanted to make it special for her. She's certainly been through enough in the past year, he recollected, even if he did try to shield her from as much as possible. Still, he knew there had been incidents: some things had been said by Katie's classmates, and some of her friends no longer came around after the trouble at Wharton. She'd borne it well, but Moses knew his sensitive daughter well enough to know that his troubles had left their marks. The move to Atlanta should prove a God-send, Moses mused, even if Katie wasn't crazy about the idea initially. It would be a little rough at the beginning starting all over again in a new city.

"If I could get through the past year, though, I should be able to do just about anything," he thought. "Miss Taylor used to call my musing wool gathering when I did it in class. She'd always ask, 'Are you planning to knit an Afghan when you're through?'"

"Earth calling Dad." Katie had returned and her throaty voice pulled Moses back from his reverie. He smiled inwardly; more than once, women of his acquaintance who had not met Katie had greeted him frostily after she answered the phone. Only after they learned that the voice was his adolescent daughter had their tone thawed. It was a marvel, that voice, coming as it did from a youngster who stood less than five feet tall and who couldn't decide yet which was more exciting, tennis or boys. Quickly, Moses put away any thoughts of women. That did nothing but evoke thoughts of the last time he had seen Maggie, his close friend clad in prison gray, her face drawn but still defiantly beautiful.

"Just thinking about all we have to do this week, honey," Moses replied. "We've got to move in when the van comes tomorrow, and then we must get the house in order. Of course, I must do the same with the office. We're going to be pretty busy for a few days, so I guess we'd better enjoy ourselves tonight. I forgot to tell you, Chuck and Barbara Ann want us to come over for dinner Friday night."

"I'd like that," Katie said. "How long has it been since I've seen them? Years and years. I remember the last time. They gave me Nemo. You're not going to tell them what happened to him, are you?"

Nemo was a stuffed lamb that the Morgans had given Katie. A smile flickered briefly across Moses' face as he remembered how his wife, who hated nicknames, had insisted that her daughter was not going to have to suffer through life with one. Thus, they named her Katie not Katherine from which the nickname is derived. Their one visit to Philadelphia had, indeed, been years ago, and it had been a grand reunion of two old friends. It seemed they'd relived almost every one of their moments at Harvard, where both had earned MBAs. Moses had been on the top of the heap at the time of that visit: a Distinguished Professor at Wharton, almost a sure shot for a marketing chair at the next vacancy, and a lucrative consulting business in marketing on the side.

Then the long nightmare had begun. For a time, he was looked down upon with disdain and suspicion by his marketing colleagues. But the plagiarizing charge that had begun his long fall into desolation had been proved false. Even though Moses' name had been totally cleared, the damage to his business relationships was irreversible.

That numbing episode was all behind him now, and it was Chuck, with his undistinguished but stable job in the overseas development arm of Coca-Cola, who had come to his rescue after Moses' troubles had caused him to leave his former position. Good old solid, plodding Chuck, who'd wrangled Moses his new teaching post at Georgia State University for the fall, who had found him the small bungalow he and Katie would be renting, and who owned the small office building where Moses would set up shop. Chuck had already gotten him his first commission, a small consulting job at the Coca-Cola division where Chuck worked.

Chuck wanted Moses to perform a marketing analysis without the word getting out to many people. It wasn't exactly hush-hush, as Moses understood it, but Chuck did want the project kept quiet. Moses had experience in uncovering foul-play during some of his previous consulting jobs. He wondered if that was the case here. The job was small potatoes compared to the not-so-distant days when Moses was a consultant to several major international corporations, but Moses was grateful both for the work and for the confidence his friend had shown in him.

"We'd better get started if we're going to take in everything at Stone Mountain before the light show tonight," Moses told his daughter as he beckoned for the check. The two had planned to see the huge granite mountain east of Atlanta as their one day of fun before buckling down for a couple of weeks of getting their new home into shape. Atlanta's other attractions--the Cyclorama, zoo, the High Museum, the state Capitol -- would have to wait till later. But Moses wanted to give his daughter at least a taste of the delights the Southern metropolis held, and Stone Mountain seemed to be the best way to do that.

His judgment turned out to be eminently correct. They were awed by the huge carving of Southern heroes Robert E. Lee, Stonewall Jackson, and Jefferson Davis that graced the side of the mountain. They had fun riding the train, visiting the game ranch, seeing the old car museum, and oohing at the laser light show. The two returned to the hotel that night tired but enthusiastic over what their new home held in store. Moses was amused and grateful, but just a little wary, when he noticed how much Katie's attitude toward the move improved when she met a group of teen-age boys at the Stone Mountain park lake, where they relaxed with a dip in the cool water for an hour or two.

"I guess a parent hasn't done his job right if he doesn't eventually render himself unnecessary," Moses mused before he drifted off to sleep. "But that doesn't make it any easier."

* * *

The next few days were a blur of scrubbing, sweeping, vacuuming, mopping, waxing, washing windows, moving furniture, moving it back again, hanging pictures, painting, mowing, pulling weeds, and all the other multitudinous tasks involved in setting up housekeeping. The bungalow had been unoccupied for the past year and half, while it was tied up in an estate, and the long vacancy showed. Southern cobwebs seemed to flourish more than their Northern cousins, Moses noted. Katie worked right beside him without complaining, but Moses knew it was an inauspicious introduction to her new home, and he made it a point to give her frequent breaks while he himself kept plugging away.

The house was smaller than either he or Katie was accustomed, and Moses didn't care much for the idea of renting. It wasn't that he was unable to buy. Moses was far from being on the dole. But with the uncertainties of starting a new firm in a new city, he thought it best to husband his resources for a year or two. Besides, he wanted the opportunity to get to know Atlanta and environs before settling down in a permanent residence. There would be plenty of time to buy after the Philadelphia place sold. The tax code allows a homeowner two years to reinvest sale proceeds in another home before taxing any gain from the sale of a residence. Moses figured that within that period he could find a place he and Katie could turn into a real home.

Several times, Moses called a halt while he went to his nearby office. That, too, had to be shaped up, and Moses didn't have the heart to ask Katie for help. The same van that had brought the McDonald household goods had brought enough of the furnishings from his former office in Philadelphia to equip the new quarters in Atlanta. Though he wasn't confronted with the same housecleaning chores that awaited him at home, Moses still had to interview for a secretary, get his telephones hooked up, and unpack his library and electronic gear. He always prided himself on having the best and latest in computer technology and on knowing how to use it.

By the time Friday afternoon arrived, the house was sparkling and had begun to feel like a home. The office was also ready, expectantly waiting his arrival Monday morning. He and Katie knocked off, ready for the dinner with the Morgans and the weekend of visiting Atlanta attractions that Moses had promised.

Moses even had time to browse through the latest copy of *The Journal of Professional Services Marketing*. One article in particular caught his eye. The author, Steve McDaniel, contended that business firms have long recognized that advertising is only one part of the "promotion mix," and promotion is only one element in the overall "marketing mix." Not only is it important to offer a good product or service at the right price, and make it available at the right time and place, but it must be promoted correctly. Moses could relate to that statement. His professional services certainly had not been well promoted this past year.

* * *

"Got the office all ship-shape? Ready to hit the ground running Monday?" Chuck Morgan asked Moses. The two old friends were relaxing in the den as Chuck's wife and Katie were cleaning up after a home cooked meal. Seeing Chuck and Barbara Ann interacting during dinner caused Moses to recall memories of his late wife. He and Katie were still struggling with their loss.

"Well, I'm ready to hit the ground, but I suspect it'll be more of a jog than a run," Moses replied. "When a fellow reaches my age, the only time he runs is when something's chasing him."

"I know I've said this before, Chuck," Moses continued, "but I do want you to know I appreciate everything you've done. If you hadn't been so insistent, I probably would have gone on moping in Philadelphia forever. I know you've gone out on a limb, and I'm grateful."

"Hey, I haven't done anything except to recommend that we hire the best consultant I know to do a little snooping for my division. You're a natural, one of the best experts around on international business and information technology. Anyway, all it took was to bring the boss home for one of Barbara Ann's pot roasts and he was sold. Of course, I did have to hook a couple of shots at the club before we got home for dinner, but you're worth it."

Chuck continued, "Did you hire that secretary I recommended?"

"Yes, and it looks like she'll do a great job. She got tired of driving a 30-mile round trip into town every day. So she's willing to give up a good job with Proctor & Gamble to be closer to home and work for me. Traffic must really be a rascal here in Atlanta if she's willing to take a pay cut to avoid the traffic jams. She knows it will be a while before she'll be getting the salary she had with them."

"Once you have the dubious opportunity to drive in Atlanta's five o'clock traffic, you'll understand why she feels that way. The only thing I can think of that's worse is being stuck in the Omni when one of those heavy metal groups is tearing the place up. Makes me just about as nervous as being tied up on the Northeast Expressway."

Chuck frowned, "Let me fill you in, though, on what to expect at the office when you start giving us the famous McDonald Meltdown. As you know, we're not expecting a full-scale operational audit. But the boss thinks we need somebody with a knowledge of business and computers to come in to make sure nothing is amiss."

"I'm asking you to constructively criticize our marketing procedures, quality control, and data processing procedures," Chuck said airily. "Normally, all my division handles is the identification and initial development of overseas markets. It's up to us to keep up with what's going on around the globe, with an eye toward what will make a buck or two for Coke. Once a specified number of the citizens of an underdeveloped nation reach a given income level, for example, it's up to my folks to know about it, and research the possibility of opening up the market for Coke."

"Demographics are one indicator of market potential, but Coke analyzes several factors which reflect a country's attractiveness as a market. We look at technological factors such as existing production and consumption technology. The geographics of the country, like population concentration, are surveyed along with sociocultural factors such as values and lifestyle patterns. A country's economy must be outlined, specifically its income distribution and gross national product growth. Just as important, or maybe more so, is the country's political-legal environment. We must consider the country's attitude toward foreign trade and any monetary regulations which affect Coke's ability to take profits out of the country. Oh, we also have to make sure that we haven't ticked off any political prima donnas, or if we have, to sweet-talk them back into good relations so we can set up a bottling plant on their front lawn."

"Internally, my division uses microcomputers for our housekeeping chores. All of our demographics work is done on one of the company's mid-size computers...that kind of data-shuffling requires a lot of horsepower. I'm not one of your whiz kids on computers, so if I'm not speaking the lingo right, just overlook it."

"What's happened is that something has come up that could be an embarrassment to the division, or at least to the Senior Vice President of Marketing in more ways than one." Chuck frowned.

Chuck thought for a moment and continued. "Mike's a good executive; I've never worked for anyone more talented. However, he does have a moral lapse every now and then. His career has suffered for it, not to mention his personal life. Here a little while back, he got involved with one of the women in the office; apparently it all started with some 'innocent' flirting which unfortunately led to something more serious. What made it even more stupid for Mike is that her husband works for the division, too. One day, she's really bent out of shape with her husband. He'd promised her a new car and bought a bass boat instead, and she tells Mike the guy is using the computer to play songs it's not supposed to play."

Chuck paused, then resumed his monologue. "Exactly what, she wouldn't or couldn't say, but she did know he'd paid cash for that boat. The lady cashes her husband's paycheck, so she knew he shouldn't have that kind of money. The problem is, Mike can't confront the thing directly. The lady and her husband are back on great terms again... close as a mama kangaroo and her joey."

"So you suspect fraud." Moses suggested. "What you need is

some exploratory research," he said, as he took the manila folder.

"Exactly what do you mean by exploratory? How deep are you going to drill?" Chuck asked, as he cocked an eyebrow.

"That's a good question but it's not easy to answer. The textbooks define exploratory research as seeking insights into the general nature of a problem, the possible decision alternatives, and relevant variables. In exploratory research, there usually isn't much prior knowledge upon which to build. Research methods must be flexible, instructive, and qualitative, since there are no solid preconceptions as to what will be found. The absence of structure permits a thorough pursuit of interesting ideas and clues. Furthermore, as in oil and gas exploration, I'm likely to hit a few dry holes."

Chuck interrupted Moses' lecture, "Gee whiz, are you always this technical? I almost forgot to tell you, there's another complication. Mike's on a fast track at the company, and he can't afford any kind of problem in his division that causes problems for other divisions. The mid-size we use also handles part of Coke's accounting system. The billings to all of our bottlers are on the mid-size, along with several miscellaneous operations. Some of the canned juice billings, for example, are on the system, and have been for about two years. And it handles many of the accounts payable for several divisions. That's temporary. Ultimately, they're to be switched over to another part of the company, but the Syrup Set--that's what we call the accounting division that handles the syrup accounts--has got 'em for now."

"Who does the billings for the bottlers themselves?" Moses asked. "Are those all franchises, or are some of them company-owned, and if they are, do they do their billing locally?"

"Hmmmmm...I forgot you're not an Atlantan," Chuck smiled. "Historically, the Coca-Cola Company does very little bottling. Let me give you some history."

"The first Coke bottler was Joseph Biedenharn, a soda fountain operator in Vicksburg, Mississippi. That was in 1894. Then in 1897, two lawyers in Chattanooga, Tennessee, persuaded Coca-Cola President Asa Candler to give them the rights to bottle and sell Coca-Cola throughout the United States, except for Mississippi, Texas, and five New England states. The lawyers were Benjamin Franklin Thomas and Joseph Brown Whitehead. They were the real beginning of the franchise system that dominated Coke for almost a century, and they got a bargain. They paid only one dollar for the bottling rights."

"That was the bargain of the century," Moses commented.

"Yeah. They paid less than today's cost of a two-liter bottle of Coke. Coke's got one of the most interesting corporate histories around. It all began with an Atlanta pharmacist, John S. Pemberton. He registered a trademark for 'French Wine Cola - ideal nerve and tonic stimulant.' His first advertisement appeared in the Atlanta *Constitution* in May 1886--'Delicious and Refreshing.' The concoction was wine allegedly mixed with--get this--cocaine. The next year Pemberton deleted the wine and added caffeine and a kola nut extract. He changed the name to Coca-Cola, and peddled it as 'brain food.' I remember one 1892 ad. It described Coke as 'The great brain and nerve tonic. Makes a pleasant and refreshing drink and is certain relief for some forms of headache.'"

"There are a lot of teenagers, including my own, who'll be glad to hear it's a brain tonic," Moses chuckled.

"There's more," Chuck continued." Asa Candler was another guy who got a bargain with Coca-Cola. He was an Atlanta businessman, and in 1891 he bought all the rights to Coke from Pemberton for $2,300. Candler began selling the syrup to wholesalers, who sold it to drugstores to be mixed with carbonated water and sold at soda fountains. In 1919, the company was sold for $25 million."

"Coca-Cola recently has been buying up its bottlers through a separate subsidiary called Coca-Cola Enterprises. Coke owns 49 percent of that operation. We're trying to consolidate. In 1950 there were more than a thousand bottlers. By 1990, they'd been reduced to 184, and we plan to continue to consolidate. The dramatic consolidation accelerated in 1986 when tax laws prompted families to sell bottling interests."

Chuck shifted on the light blue couch and spoke again. "But let's get back to our immediate problem. What Mike is worried about most is Little Willie. That's Willie Butler Buford, Jr., who heads up the syrup crew. He and Mike go way back, which is where Little Willie would like to send Mike. They're old college classmates, and there hasn't been a good feeling between them since Mike put a dead snake in Little Willie's bed one night, and Little Willie actually wet his pants in front of half the Dartmouth polo team. Mike's quite a one for pranks. Unfortunately, Little Willie's even bigger on grudges than Mike is on pranks. He'd love to nail Mike's hide to the office door of the vice president for operations."

"That's why, if there's any hanky-panky going on with the computers, Mike's got to get a fix on it first. That way he not only can head off Little Willie, but he can actually come out looking good...like he's on top of things. So, for reasons of secrecy and urgency, we're calling in some trustworthy outside help, namely you."

"I'll do my best," Moses promised.

"That's always been good enough for me," Chuck replied. "C'mon, let's go bore the girls with more of the old college days. And for goodness sake, don't mention that episode with Debbie Dallas when we were first-year graduate students. She and her husband live in Atlanta now, and I don't want to give Barbara Ann the idea that the flame's still burning."

Chapter 2

It's fair to say price is now probably the least effective arrow in your marketing quiver. Jaded consumers don't believe words like "manufacturers's list price," "discount," or even "sale" anymore.

Paul B. Brown

Moses was in the office by 7:30 a.m. Monday with a pot of coffee brewing, and was on his second cup when his new secretary arrived. Doris Lawrence was an attractive woman, no doubt about it, but Moses was not one of those executives who wanted just a pretty face at the front desk. He wanted competence, loyalty, and confidence, and he had gotten exactly that when he hired Doris. Judging by her recommendations, Doris' former employers were aware she wanted to find something closer to home, and had willingly, but with obvious regret, given her the highest recommendations. Furthermore, she suffused the whole office with the cheeriness of a field of daisies.

"It's going to be pretty slow around here for the first couple of days," Moses said as he was packing his briefcase, "so if you've got any personal correspondence to catch up on, now's the time. All we need to do right now is finish putting up the books and do whatever straightening up that's necessary."

"This may be the easiest job I ever had," Doris said with a perky smile.

"Well, there is one other thing that should occupy you for a little while," Moses noted. "Have you ever used this software before?" The professor pointed to a stack of manuals at least 24 inches high.

Doris quickly examined them. "I know Windows, of course," she said. "But the word processing program is different from the one we used at Proctor & Gamble. So is the spreadsheet program. The Compaq is also new to me."

"These are all current releases," Moses said. "This software will do everything we're going to need to do for a long time to come. Tell you what, plan to spend your time getting to be the most proficient operator in Atlanta on this setup. Then, when things start picking up, we'll be off to a running start. If you need me, I'll be at this number. Just ask for Chuck Morgan, and he can track me down."

* * *

Based on the map, the trip to the Coca-Cola headquarters in downtown Atlanta from suburban Sandy Springs was a fairly direct one, using Roswell Road. Direct it was; quick it wasn't. Moses got his first taste of the storied Atlanta traffic, a taste that threw him a quarter of an hour late. He noticed that Georgia Tech University was across the street from Coke. He didn't like being late, because Moses McDonald was always on time, and his usually equable temperament was somewhat frayed when he finally arrived at Chuck's office.

The Coke executive was an old friend of Moses, but that didn't make him feel any better about being late. As a veteran of years in the Atlanta traffic trenches, Chuck was understanding and a trifle amused at his friend's discomfort. He quickly restored Moses's equanimity and took him to an available office where they discussed the case.

"First," explained Chuck, "let me give you some pertinent background information on the Coca-Cola Company. Big changes have recently been made in the organization of the marketing department. The changes were the result of an eight month company-wide study. Even an industry leader like Coca-Cola must be flexible and able to adapt to environmental changes. The global marketplace is extremely competitive. Many organizations undergo periodic structural changes as they experiment with varying degrees of centralization that shift decision-making authority. The eventual complexity of the structure will be determined not by size but by interaction between people and organizational goals."

"Coca-Cola has traditionally been organized according to brand management where the manager's job is to develop and implement a complete strategy and marketing program for a specific brand or product. With the recent changes, the brand management responsibilities have been narrowed to focus on strategy, while the new organizational areas will concentrate on implementation. Some tasks have become centralized (most decisions are made by one person or committee) versus decentralized (decision making is spread throughout the organization)."

"For example, the brand managers were responsible for the advertising and promotion of their own brands and this required direct contact with ad agencies for that purpose. That function and contact now has been centralized--there is a new group of staff-support positions. Coca-Cola has a director of advertising plus a director of marketing services. The director of marketing services, Linda Barfoot, is responsible for promotion, media, packaging, and the vending market. While brand managers develop strategy, the functional departments will implement the programs. In short, the consumer marketing activities in various departments have been consolidated and realigned in the marketing department. The synergy of these functions is expected to create a more focused environment for the total marketing effort. Of course, real organizations seldom run as orderly as the organizational charts portray. The charts fail to show the overlapping or overlooked responsibilities, informal communication lines, personal conflicts, or uncertainties. Sometimes the imperfections seem overwhelming, but if we work together and use a little resourcefulness, we can be successful."

"Because of these changes, the vice-presidents around here are extra sensitive to any operational problems occurring right now. So we're counting on you to quietly investigate the current indiscretion."

Moses felt this job would not be too difficult. Chuck and his boss suspected only one person of improper practices. Thus, Moses could confine his review, at least initially, to the activities of the suspect. He might have to give the appearance of a broader research, just to avoid tipping off any inquisitive and particularly observant employees, but the inquiry would still target just one individual.

The suspect was Chris Ray Brown. From all outward appearances, Chris was an unlikely candidate to be playing games with Coca-Cola's corporate checkbook. He had been with Coke for 19 years, beginning as a computer operator in payroll. After taking college courses at night and obtaining a bachelors degree in marketing, he had worked himself up to the point where he was in charge of sales management for the international division.

Moses began his investigation by conferring with the head of accounting. Moses asked for a copy of last year's audit report. The chief accountant felt compelled to first explain what a financial audit by a CPA firm entailed.

"First, the independent auditor, i.e., public accountant, plans the audit. This step includes gathering information about the client's firm and industry conditions. Second, the auditor studies, tests, and evaluates the client firm's control structure. Third, the auditor performs and evaluates substantive tests. A substantive test is used to determine whether an account balance such as inventory is correctly stated on the financial statements. The second and third steps are the evidence-gathering steps of the audit. Audit working papers are used to document the auditor's techniques. Based upon this evidence, the auditor completes the fourth and final essential step, issuing the audit report."

"Here's one of our previous audit reports."

Board of Directors and Shareholders
The Coca-Cola Company
Atlanta, Georgia

We have audited the accompanying consolidated balance sheets of Coca-Cola Company and its subsidiaries as of December 31, 1998 and 1997, and the related consolidated statements of income, share-owners equity, and cash flows for the three years in the period ended December 31, 1998. These financial statements are the responsibility of the Company's management. Our responsibility is to express an opinion on these financial statements based on our audits.

We conducted our audits in accordance with generally accepted auditing standards. Those standards require that we plan and perform the audit to obtain reasonable assurance about whether the financial statements are free of material misstatement. An audit includes examining, on a test basis, evidence supporting the amounts and disclosures in the financial statements. An audit also includes assessing the accounting principles used and significant estimates made by management, as well as evaluating the overall financial statement presentation. We believe that our audits provide a reasonable basis for our opinion.

In our opinion, the financial statements referred to above present fairly, in all material respects, the consolidated financial position of Coca-Cola Company and its subsidiaries at December 31, 1998 and 1997, and the consolidated results of their operations and their cash flows for each of the three years in the period ended December 31, 1998, in conformity with generally accepted accounting principles.

Ernst & Young
February 1, 1999

The chief accountant continued, "As you can see, this standard report includes what is referred to as an `unqualified opinion', which basically means that the financial statements are fairly presented. In other words, Coca-Cola was given a clean bill of health."

Moses knew that conditions may prevent an independent auditor from following generally accepted auditing standards (GAAS) or that auditors might find something during the audit to stop them from reporting that the financial statements are fair and in accordance with generally accepted accounting principles (GAAP). Thus, three other types of reports may be issued: a qualified opinion, a disclaimer, or an adverse opinion. Various websites provide information about audit reporting (e.g. http://acct.tamu.edu/Smith/audport/intro.htm).

Two reasons may cause an auditor to issue a *qualified* opinion. First, something may prevent an auditor from performing all of the necessary audit procedures (e.g. the auditor being unable to examine records of a foreign subsidiary or to observe the inventory count). This is referred to as a scope limitation. Second, the auditor may decide that the company did not follow GAAP (e.g. the company improperly computing the value of inventory).

When financial statements are not presented fairly in accordance with GAAP, an auditor will issue an adverse or qualified opinion. Whether to use a qualified or adverse opinion depends on the extent to which the departure from GAAP affects the overall financial statements. An adverse opinion is extremely rare. On the other hand, when an auditor lacks the knowledge to form any opinion on the financial statements, a disclaimer of opinion is appropriate. This type of audit report may be used when the auditor lacks sufficient evidence to form an opinion.

The chief accountant explained to Moses that being an accounting professional required far more than just a textbook understanding of debits and credits, journalizing and posting steps, and the latest accounting and auditing pronouncements. The accounting professional must also stay abreast of the many technological advances which continually reshape the business world. Modern technology permits, for example, the rapid processing of huge volumes of transactions, the immediate updating of on-line files, point-of-sale (POS) transaction entry, rapid access to data in integrated databases, instantaneous data communications within geographically distributed computer networks, and an increased level of computer resource sharing. To a decision maker this translates into more accurate, reliable, and timely information to support tough economic decisions made in an ever more competitive environment. This enhances planning and control at all organizational levels and for all aspects of business activity.

The function of the accounting information system (AIS) is to provide, in a timely and effective manner, all the financial information needed by managers, throughout the organization, so that they can make the best possible decisions. The accounting information system is one component of the firm's management information system (MIS) which is responsible for providing all information, financial and nonfinancial, needed for decision-making within the organization.

The chief accountant told Moses that Coke had an internal auditing department which regularly conducted operational audits. Operational audits had different objectives than the financial statement audits which were conducted by a CPA firm. Coke was required by the federal securities laws to have an annual external audit of its financial statements. A CPA firm was hired as an independent contractor to conduct the external audit.

Unlike the external auditors of a CPA firm, internal auditors are employees of Coke. Operational audits are broader in scope than financial statement audits. Operational audits are concerned with determining whether a firm is achieving its goals and objectives, these may include financial and nonfinancial items. For example, a firm's goals might include increasing revenues and profits, but also include items such as improving customer satisfaction, developing new products or services, and participating in special community projects.

Moses next interviewed the supervisor of overseas development. Moses explained that the division was looking at its computer requirements, and asked for a brief outline of the operations the supervisor needed the computer to do. He got more than he requested. The supervisor stressed the uncertainties and risks he dealt with in planning overseas development. A large part of his job dealt with risk management, the process of using information to identify and reduce risk indecisions. Some uncertainties can be controlled if management has access to information that can predict the behavior of relevant variables. Of course, some external uncertainties, such as the possibility of worldwide recession, will always remain uncontrollable. However, the recession may be predicted, and decisions can be made to reduce company risk. In a decision, a fact qualifies as information if awareness of it could change a manager's preference among alternatives.

For 45 minutes, Moses listened to a long and exquisitely detailed explanation of the needs for the overseas development crew, and a string of complaints about the low priority it had been assigned for computer equipment.

"In overseas development, I need the latest computer technology to operate our financial planning model. A financial planning model is a set of equations that describes, in monetary terms, the relationships between an organization and its environment and the changes that occur in these relationships as time passes. The model allows me to explore the financial effects of varying sets of economic conditions and operating policies. A computerized model can handle a wider range of assumptions and strategies at a quicker rate. It can apply formulas to calculate forecasted values of variables such as product price, unit sales, productivity, and material costs. I need this information to identify production goals which serve as a starting point for future budget preparations."

Moses finally managed to rid himself of the overzealous executive, but not before he had been promised "a complete draft of his ongoing and vastly expanded needs." Moses pledged to review the draft carefully, and gratefully ushered the visitor out the door.

The next two interviews went more swiftly, and by 11:30 Moses was ready to talk to Chris, who all along had been the only one in whom Moses was really interested. The other interviews had only been smoke screens that Moses hoped would allay any suspicions regarding the true target of the investigation. He wanted to get a first-hand look at Chris. Face-to-face conferences were not a required investigative tool, but Moses had more than once learned that taking personal measure of an adversary could be productive. He wished he had a second person to help in the interview to listen and act as a witness.

"I guess Mike explained that we're taking a look at the division's computer requirements," Moses said as he ushered Chris into the small office. "This is just a preliminary meeting to give me some grasp of what your current duties are. We'll be going into a lot more depth later, and you'll be talking with other consultants in more detail. I have some computer expertise, but I want to be sure of the procedures you have in place so I'll know what changes are indicated, if any. How about giving me a quick run-down on how you handle your end of things."

Chris quickly launched into an explanation of his duties. "Salesforce management is the analysis, planning, implementation, and control of salesforce activities. Thus, my job includes stating salesforce objectives and strategies. I also oversee the recruiting, training, and supervising of our salespeople. We adhere to the new market-oriented view of selling -- that is, salespeople must produce both customer satisfaction and company profit." Chris then told Moses about their record-keeping system and how the computer played an integral part. It was all very general, Moses noted, except that Chris did seem to dwell a trifle long on the safeguards included in the record-keeping system. On the other hand, he reflected, perhaps I'm just being overly suspicious.

Moses knew that body language was important in any interview or interrogation. An innocent person will sit upright in the chair, maintain strong eye contact, and give quick answers and denials. He or she may become angry or hostile. A guilty person may be more passive, playing a cat and mouse game with false clues. Untruthful answers may cause dry mouth and lips, that result in a clicking sound when speaking. A dishonest person may avoid eye contact, or stare at the interviewer and then drop the eyes down or away as they answer a question. Restlessness and shifting in a chair, abnormal eye-blink rate, and biting of the lips or tongue are other tell-tale signs of dishonest answers. One must observe both verbal and nonverbal signals during the exploratory process.

Moses wrapped up the interview just before lunch, as he had planned. He'd wanted to listen to and take a measure of Chris, not answer any questions. Thus, the timing of the interview was part of Moses's plan. It gave Moses the excuse to cut off discussion when he'd sized up the suspect.

Moses had made previous arrangements to meet Chuck at the Diplomat in downtown Atlanta. It was unlikely that anybody else from the division would be frequenting that restaurant, Chuck had explained, and lunch would give them time to review the morning's events.

"Looks like you're becoming a veteran of Atlanta traffic already," Chuck grinned, sliding a Coke toward Moses as he eased into a chair. "You're only seven minutes late."

"I am reminded of the injunction, 'All things come to him who waits,'" Moses sighed. "I hope so, because it seems I'll be spending a large part of my life from now on waiting in mini-traffic jams."

"Don't worry about it. You may be late but you're impeccably dressed."

Moses laughed. "What can I say, Chuck? The consultant's dress code is a dark, preferably pin-striped, suit. Let's face it, clients trust conservatively dressed people. Besides, I've noticed you business executives 'dress for success' the same way." Moses paused to smile. "At least I look like I know what I'm doing." Both men grinned at Moses's self-depreciation.

"How's it going in the office?" Chuck queried. "Found any skunks in any woodpiles?"

"Skunks would be a lot easier to find!" Moses said with a grin. "I've talked to your man Chris Ray Brown, along with a couple of other chaps. He seems cool enough. Certainly is ready to convince you that internal controls are close to foolproof. And that's without even being asked."

"So what's next on the agenda?"

"Well, I've got one more interview set up for this afternoon. It isn't necessary, but I don't want to spook Chris. This way, I'm hoping he won't get the idea that I'm focusing on him. After that comes an examination of the computer records, starting with Chris' records. If we're lucky, and if there is something going on, we'll find it right off. If not, then we'll expand the scope of things."

"Good. Mike has told his secretary to provide you with any information you need. She knows just about anything you should need to know about office routine, record-keeping, the whole nine yards. Plus, she is thoroughly versed on our computer operation. She's been with Mike ever since he joined Coca-Cola. I'd stake my reputation, such as it is, on her discretion, and so would Mike. In fact, considering his occasional philandering, he probably has."

"Good," Moses replied, just as the prime rib arrived. "I'll need her help this afternoon, as soon as I finish with this final interview. That's when we'll start actually trying to determine what Chris has been up to, if anything."

* * *

When Moses returned to the Coke building, he first reviewed

Coke's marketing information system (Marketing IS) to get a feel for how the company operated. As with any good marketing IS, Coke's consisted of people, equipment, and procedures to gather, sort, analyze, evaluate, and distribute information to marketing decision makers. The trick is in balancing the information the managers would like to have against what they really need and what is feasible to provide. With Ms. Trueblood's help, Moses sorted through recent internal records, marketing intelligence reports, and marketing research.

Two hours later, Moses was ready to zero in on Chris' computer records. Since there were far too many records to look at individually, Moses took a probability sample in which all population members (computer records) have a known probability of being in the sample. The simplest way to select a probability sample is termed "simple random sampling" in which each population member has an equal probability of being selected.

Moses recalled how simple random sampling was used to select the order in which men would be drafted during the Vietnam War, using birth dates. The names of each person in the population (men eligible for war) were put in a bowl. The initial drawing revealed a much higher number of names with late birth dates, such as December, rather than early dates, such as January. The apparent reason was that the names with December birth dates were put in last and the bowl could not be mixed sufficiently to create a random draw. The solution was to randomize the order in which the dates were put in the bowl.

To draw a random sample from Chris' computer records, Moses used an inquiry program which randomly selected the first record and then systematically pulled every tenth record for the past two years. This method of simple random sampling is termed "systematic sampling." Moses compared each record with the actual paperwork. He was looking for differences between computer entries and the paper trail left by the division's record-keeping. If Chris was as astute as he had appeared in the interview, Moses knew the rifle-shot approach would be a long shot, but it was worth a try. As things turned out, that's all it ended up being -- just a try. The computer entries tallied perfectly with the accompanying paperwork.

Moses had been looking for one dodge in particular; it had seemed a likely chance after he had done some initial comparisons. All the data entered on the timekeeping and payroll system on the computer carried both the employee's name and his employee number. Manually, though, all processing and control was based on the employee's name alone. The reverse was true for the computerized system. All the processing was done by numbers. The computer even used numbers, without any reference to employees' names, to look up names and addresses to print payroll checks.

Anyone with larcenous intent could have used that information in several fashions to feather his nest, Moses knew. He recalled one case in Harrisburg, Pennsylvania where a supervisor had filled out fake overtime forms for employees, but entered his own employee number in the computer.

Obviously, Chris had not been sticking his hand in the Coca-Cola till through that particular loophole. Moses was back at square one.

Chapter 3

When Frederick Koch got tired of having his name mispronounced, he legally changed it to "Coke-Is-It." Coca- Cola's attempt to legally stop him failed.

John Koten

The crystal octagon continued its halting but unvarying revolutions. Ninety degrees, then a pause while a right index finger absently stroked the chilled dew from the sloping facet of the glass. About every revolution and a half, the glass rose, tilted a fraction of Pepsi across the waiting lips, then descended to resume the circling libational ballet that had begun almost an hour before. Although he would not tell his current employer, sometimes he liked arch-rival Pepsi better than Coke.

Moses McDonald was in one of his famous abstracted moods, what Katie called his "terminal trances," oblivious to all around him. Not that there was much with which to be oblivious. Katie had already gone to bed, and Moses had never been much of one for background music or television. The house was quiet, with only the muted rumble of the Roswell Road traffic intruding on its silence. He was breaking his personal rule, never to drink caffeine after nine o'clock in the evening. Three hours from now he would be wide awake. For some reason he remembered the fact that a bottle of soda contains approximately one-fourth the amount of caffeine as a cup of brewed coffee, and about one-third that of tea.

He was mulling over the day's events. The Coca-Cola case was not going badly. By any measure, it was far too early to make that judgment. But Moses did want to wrap it up with a minimum of expense to his client. He wanted the company's divisional superintendent as a reference later, and the quicker he could get to the bottom of matters at the soft-drink company, the greater the likelihood of a glowing reference. That meant either he needed a lot of luck in identifying any misuse or misappropriation of funds or goods, or he needed to zero in on the process that was being misused. Moses McDonald had never been one to trust anything to luck. That left only one other alternative--raw intelligence combined with applied knowledge. Thus the deep contemplation.

He had already eliminated two possible scams in the past hour. One was the inventory salami technique. Though not particularly sophisticated, this technique had proved effective many times for the larcenously inclined, Moses knew. Someone with appropriate access randomly reduces inventories by a tiny fraction of what each totals, and then reallocates the goods to another account within the system. The goods are then drawn down. Because the inventory is simply rearranged within the system, no controls are breached. The losses to each account are so minimal they either go unnoticed or unreported. Such scams also work moderately well with large numbers of accounts held by many people, as in the banking system. In the case of Coke's international division, though, Moses knew that the inventory was so spread out that the amount housed in Atlanta was insufficient to generate any substantial amount of cash. About all a thief could get would be enough Cokes to supply a middle-sized Fourth of July party.

The other technique he felt could be eliminated was the round-down. Such schemes required great numbers of accounts that involved percentage chargeables or payables, such as credit cards or savings accounts. Frequently, when a sum is multiplied by the required percentage, the result is less than a full cent. In round-downs, the swindler randomly chooses a number of the accounts to round down to the nearest cent. The fraction of a cent then goes into a separate account to which he has access. The customer loses nothing, since he would not have received the fraction of a cent anyway, and he is never the wiser. With large numbers of accounts, the technique can add up to large sums being misappropriated. But, just as in the salami technique, Coke simply did not have the volume of accounts required for such a scam to pay off.

"No, the fraudulent technique had to be something else, something quite simple and direct, probably some weekly or monthly expense incurred by the division that would be obvious once spotted," thought Moses. "Possibly it is one that would surface in a full-scale investigation, but I have to find it a lot quicker than that."

"Perhaps I'm overlooking an involvement with the marketing intermediaries, the firms that help promote, sell, and distribute Coca-Cola products to the final buyers." Mentally, he went through the list. "There's the middlemen -- that is, wholesalers and retailers -- who make the sales to the customers. There's the physical distribution firms who aid in stocking and moving the product. These are the warehouse and transportation firms. Then there's the marketing services agencies who help Coca-Cola target the right markets and promote its products. This group includes research firms, ad agencies, media firms, and consultants like me. Last, but not least, there's financial institutions that help finance and insure against risk."

The glass paused midway in one of its upward swings, then slowly drifted downward again. The revolutions stopped, then resumed again abruptly for a 180 degree turn before the glass swiftly made a full trip back up. Moses, the faraway look gone, swished down the last of the Pepsi, then strode to the sink and dumped the ice. With a smile of obvious satisfaction, he flipped off the light on the way to his bedroom for what he wished would be a night of sound sleep.

* * *

Chuck was right. Mike's secretary knew her business -- and just about everybody else's, too.

"Do all the employees of the international division work here in Atlanta?" Moses asked her after he had settled into his temporary cubicle in the Coke building the next morning.

"Oh, no," the secretary quickly replied. "We have quite a few who work elsewhere. There are several in New York, for example, who work out of the offices of another Coke division there, though we have jurisdiction over them. There is a small branch in Los Angeles that takes care of much of the Asian market. And, of course, at any given time we'll have operatives in several foreign locations, establishing new markets. Those are permanently assigned to this office, though they may stay out-of-country for as much as a year or two."

"The New York and L.A. staff...they're permanently assigned there?" Moses asked. "How are they paid?"

"By bank transfer, I think, in every case."

"How about expenses? Do they have expense accounts? If they do, how are they paid?"

"Now that you ask, I'm not sure how they're paid," the secretary replied thoughtfully. "I know they each send in an accounting each month. I've seen those. But I'm not sure exactly how payment is handled."

"Tell you what, please pull me a hard copy of the New York and L.A. staff roster. Then let's take a look at their last few expense accounts," Moses said. It was difficult to keep the edge of excitement from his voice.

Within 15 minutes, the professor's suspicions had been confirmed. As noon approached, he called Chuck and suggested they have lunch together.

* * *

"It was simple, once I thought about it," Moses told the Coke executive as they nibbled at their salads. "It all tied back to your expense accounts. Payables to the staff... uh, salary and expenses... are all processed by name, though the employee number appears on the forms. But for the computer bookkeeping, it's all done by number. So, Brown has been submitting phony expense forms for the staffers in New York and Los Angeles. When it goes on the computer, though, he inserts his employee number. The funds have been deposited directly into a separate bank account he established."

"Since employees don't get W-2 forms or a Form 1099 for reimbursed out-of-pocket expenses, they were never aware of the scam. He was issuing two checks, one to the employee for the legitimate expenses and one to him that was direct-deposited. Brown is randomly rotating the bogus expense checks among the various out-of-town staffers. Not too sophisticated, but effective for a time."

"Good job, Moses," Chuck said enthusiastically. "I knew we'd identified the right man. Any idea how much he's gotten away with?"

"Not yet, but you're not going to be looking at any losses that will shake Coca-Cola to it's fiscal foundations," Moses replied. "This scheme is really pretty penny-ante stuff. The most I've found so far, going back about three months, is six or seven hundred dollars a month. It really depends on how long it's been going on. That isn't really the question, though."

"No?" Chuck asked, puzzled. "What else is there?"

"Well," Moses went on, choosing his words carefully. "You can cure this problem pretty easily, just by getting rid of Brown. And you can probably prevent a recurrence of this particular scam by changing your procedures slightly. One way to do that, for example, is for all computer procedures to append to each employee's number the first three letters of his surname. That way it's readily apparent to anyone who's looking, that something is awry. What bothers me is that we've caught a greedy little guppy, but you may be letting sharks into the swimming pool."

"What do you mean?" Chuck asked.

"Well... Chuck, I hope you know me well enough to know that I'm not going to start crying 'Wolf!' just to generate a little business. But your computer security is awfully loose. There have been a couple of times in the past few days that I've been astonished at the virtually unrestricted access that Angie has had. Don't get me wrong. I'm not saying Angie has done anything wrong, or has even thought about it, for that matter. She seems to be the epitome of the dedicated, loyal, and totally honest employee. But with all the data locked up in your computer, access should be tightly controlled. It should be almost like military secrets, on a `need-to-know' basis."

"So what do you suggest?" Chuck asked.

"I think you need to have someone with more expertise than me take a look at what you're doing, and see where things need to be tightened up. I'm not trying to expand the scope of what you hired me to do just to keep drawing my consultation fee. Believe me, there's a lot of potential for some major problems."

"Certainly I believe you," Chuck said with a grin. "I've not doubted you since that time you told me you could talk that blasted parakeet of mine down out of a tree after he escaped--and you did it."

"I never did tell you about the bird seed I had in the rim of my hat, did I?" Moses chuckled.

"No, you didn't," Chuck said with an incredulous laugh. "And for years I've been telling that story, about my friend with the mystical way with animals. You're nothing but a lousy con artist. To think, I'm trusting you with my company's secrets. Seriously though, what exactly do you want me to do? "

"I took the liberty of making a call this morning to an old friend who is on the faculty at Wharton now. He's a bit of a specialist in computer systems. He knows a grad student who has taken off a semester before starting on a dissertation for a Ph.D. The grad student is a computer whiz and he's right here in Atlanta. If anyone can find which buttons are available to be pushed by the wrong people, it's this fellow. His name's John Wayne Jones. They call him 'Duke' Jones. I thought you might be interested in talking to Duke, and having him take a look at the security controls you have. It may save you some major headaches down the road."

"I certainly like the idea," Chuck said thoughtfully. "Of course, we'll have to take it up with my boss, Mike Elliott. I'll set up a meeting with him for tomorrow morning. Meanwhile, these steaks deserve something better than to be ignored."

Chapter 4

Door-to-door interviewing has special risks. One researcher knocked on an apartment door while a burglary was in progress. The burglar agreed to be interviewed. The police arrived during the interview and mistakenly arrested the researcher as the burglar's accomplice.

Philip Kother and Gary Armstrong

Moses arrived at the Coke offices early the next morning in order to prepare for his meeting with Chuck and Mike Elliot. Someone he didn't know brought him a cup of coffee. That was a kind act he thought. He told the person thanks and she left with a friendly smile. As things turned out, though, he never took a sip. The coffee turned cold sitting on his desk, as he went in and out of his office double-checking the information pertinent to his meeting.

"Moses, are you ready for the shake down?" Chuck asked as he walked into the office. "My boss doesn't like to waste time."

"Ready and willing," Moses replied as he absentmindedly poured his cold coffee into a large plant pot next to his desk.

Moses and Chuck walked down the hall and into Mike Elliot's office.

"So ... what does it boil down to? On how long a ride have we been taken?" Mike Elliot, Senior Vice President of Marketing, impaled Moses and Chuck with one of his patented piercing gazes.

As Moses watched the Senior Vice President, he thought to himself. "I don't think I've ever known anyone who could simultaneously look determined and sound resigned. Of course, I don't guess I've known too many guys who've been in his shoes, either, looking at their career spiraling down the toilet because they dishonored their marital commitment. Too often people justify marriage infidelity because their spouse doesn't make them happy. I can't remember any wedding vows that went 'for better or worse or for as long as you make me happy.' Genuine commitment and honest effort could bring success to virtually any marriage."

Moses' thoughts were interrupted by Chuck's response to the

executive. "Not nearly as bad as it could be, Mike. It looks like Brown has been massaging the expense reports of the people in the New York and L.A. offices for about two and a half years now, submitting fake expense reports and having the payments deposited into an account at a Citizens and Southern branch in Fairburn. Best Moses can make out, he's snared about $19,000."

"Is he nailed?" Mike demanded. Chuck turned to Moses.

"Oh, yes, I don't think there's any question about that," Moses interposed. "We've got the account number at Fairburn C&S, where he's been making the deposits. Shouldn't be difficult at all to establish whose account it is, even if he's been using an assumed name. He's also left a wide paper trail. Some of the expense reports are obvious forgeries, once you start looking for them. I don't think there's going to be much difficulty at all in getting a conviction."

"Conviction?" Mike's voice rose a quarter-register. "Uh, well, uh, yes, that's one of the alternatives we'll have to examine, of course. Considering the nature of the case, though, we'll also have to take a look at whether it's in the company's best interest to pursue a criminal action. You know...there are a couple of considerations: the lost time from work that the witnesses would have, and the bad publicity when an employee is publicly identified as a thief. Maybe it's best just to get rid of Brown and write off the loss. Besides, we don't want to give anybody else any ideas, now, do we?"

Moses and Chuck glanced furtively at each other. "Yes, Chuck," Moses thought, "I'm reading this hand just like you. If Mike tries to ship Brown off to jail, the wife is going to raise cane, and one of the first things that she's going to raise cane about is the little fling she had with the boss. That'll cost Mike not only his job, but his wife. He's on a slippery slope. On the other hand, if he just lets the guy know what he has, he can force him to resign, get his wife transferred to another division, and let her know that if their previous cozy relationship ever surfaces, her husband is headed down river to be tailored for a striped suit. He can do it under the guise of avoiding some bad press for the company."

"Oh, I agree, Mike," Chuck said. "One thing we don't want

bandied around is that it's easy to embezzle Coke's hard-earned money. Along those lines, Moses had some interesting observations the other day. He seems to think that maybe we ought to take a closer look at all our computer security. Appears that it's not at all difficult for people to get sticky fingers, as lax as the Syrup Set has been in handling the computer processing."

"You dangle the bait so invitingly," Moses thought, "letting Mike know that maybe his old foe Little Willie has a chink in his corporate armor."

"How does that affect us?" Mike asked. "That's Willie Buford's department. Little Willie runs the syrup set, the accounting division that handles the syrup accounts. He may not want us butting into his business. However, I suppose if he's got a problem, then we need to let him know about it." Mike scowled.

"It was almost like taking a dose of castor oil for him to say that," Moses thought. "Mike and Little Willie really don't like each other. So let's see how far he's willing to go with this game of corporate one-upmanship."

"We don't know that there are any problems, Mike. Or at least any problems that have resulted in any other losses. What Moses tells me, though, is that the whole system lacks any kind of meaningful security. If that's the case, then it is our business. We've got data on that system that can't be replaced and data that we don't want to fall into the wrong hands. Moses tells me he can bring someone in for a few weeks, let him take a look at the access we have to the system, and determine if it's too unrestricted. There would be almost no contact with the accounting division. They wouldn't even have to know we're doing it. I know it would be best to wait till Little Willie ... uh, Mr. Buford ... is back from his vacation, but Moses tells me this fellow is the best, and he's only going to be available for a few weeks. He's out of Philadelphia, and as I understand it, he is here to see his folks. If anything comes of it, we'll kick it over to Mr. Buford immediately."

"You are smooth, Chuck, you silver-tongued rascal," Moses thought. "I never knew you had it in you to play these games so skillfully. He's here to see his folks, all right--for four months.

Without ever saying so, you've let Mike know he can turn this debacle with Brown into a star in his crown, if he can uncover some serious security problems in the other division. At the same time, if things are as loose over there as they seem to be with the computer system, Mike can slap it to a corporate rival like a spoiled mackerel right in the face. And he can have it all in place before Buford ever gets back into town and gets wind of anything."

Moses watched with amusement as Mike almost visibly went through the same mental scenario. Finally, the executive unfolded his hands and stood up.

"Okay, Chuck, whatever you think is best. Just don't get in anybody's hair over there on the Syrup side, and for goodness sake don't give anybody the idea we think they're running a sloppy operation. Any accessing you do, I want it to be confined as far as possible to those programs we're supposed to be screwing around with, not the Syrup Set's database. And Moses, I don't want anybody planning to buy their vacation cottage with Coca-Cola fees. Keep the time down, and keep the fees reasonable. I've got to go to a meeting downtown at the Trust Company, but I want to hear from you in a couple of days."

Turning to Chuck, Mike said, "Get Brown out of the office till 4 o'clock today. Send him on whatever errands you can find, and have Angie cut his final paycheck. Give him his accrued vacation, but no severance pay. We'll wrap up any loose ends later, but at 4 o'clock I want him and you in my office so I can personally receive his resignation. Run me a copy of several of those forged expense accounts, too. Just to make sure we got it cinched down, call one of the people in L.A. and one in New York on the latest expense accounts. Tell 'em there's been some kind of screw-up here. Go over their original submission, and verify that the bogus expenses were never incurred. Remember: 4 o'clock, with his final paycheck ready. That scheming scumbag."

"One other thing. Check the job board. See what job is available in Mrs. Brown's pay bracket for which she qualifies. I sure don't want a disgruntled wife making waves in my division."

As Moses left the office, he noticed a brightly colored book on Mike's desk. It was entitled *Coca-Cola Superstar*, by Fiora S. Palazzini. There was a Coke can with a $5 bill sticking out the top sitting on the side of his massive desk.

Outside the office Moses asked Chuck, "Why does Mike have that $5 in the Coke can on his desk?"

Chuck smiled only briefly. "That's a MagiCan. In the summer of 1990 Coke launched an innovative sales promotion with instant-win cans. A buyer would open the top of the can and out would pop either cash or certificates for prizes."

"I remember that. There were some defective cans, as I recall."

"Oh, you remember that. MagiCans were discontinued only three weeks after they were put on the shelves. The defective cans caused so much negative publicity that Coke decided to pull the plug on the MagiCans before the press got any worse. Mike keeps the can on his desk to remind him of the perils of getting carried away with an innovative promotion without thoroughly thinking it through."

"Surely you guys test-marketed the MagiCan."

"Yeah, they were test-marketed for several weeks in Illinois and Iowa the fall before they went national. Perhaps they should have been tested longer though, especially when the test markets indicated there could be problems. At least one person, that we know of, broke into a MagiCan to look at the prize contraption. Coke spent more than two years developing the technology for MagiCans. It was such an attention grabber that the people here at Atlanta headquarters were chomping at the bit to use it as the core of the summer promotion for our flagship brand, Coca-Cola Classic."

"Maybe I shouldn't admit this, but when I first saw the advertisements for the MagiCans, I didn't realize that the cash would really come out of the actual cans. I thought it was just symbolism showing that specially marked cans could be worth money."

"Actually, you're not the only one who thought that. We discovered that the concept of the MagiCans was hard for the consumer to grasp since it was so new. We had been working with the MagiCans for so long we just forgot that the average consumer would need more of an explanation than our original advertisements were giving. I guess you could say we were too close to the product. So the advertisements were reworked to stress that there really was cash in the cans."

"Wasn't there a problem with someone drinking some water from one of the MagiCans?"

"You remember that too, huh. In the first week of the promotion, an 11-year-old boy got a defective MagiCan and drank the water it contained. The water was harmless but really yucky tasting and that kid got all kinds of publicity. The MagiCans were filled with water so they would have the feel of a regular can. The water was supposedly sealed off so that no one could get to it. We at Coke thought it was such a long shot for someone to actually drink that foul-smelling water that we didn't even consider it a risk. Just goes to show that you should never underestimate the consumer!"

Chuck continued, "When Coke received over a dozen reports of cans with broken mechanisms, a massive research effort went out to discover just how many cans were broken. Of course the cans would be ruined if they were actually opened, so testers simply shook the cans and listened for rattling noises. It was determined that close to one percent of the mechanisms were broken. Immediately, full-page newspaper ads were taken out to show the consumer what a broken MagiCan looked like compared with an unbroken one. Consumers were advised not to drink the water and were given a toll-free number with which they could phone in complaints."

Moses shook his head. "What was done with the MagiCans that were already out on the market?"

"I think Coke managed to end the MagiCans in an intriguing way. The final ads were something like 'the last MagiCans are out there, but not for long...' or 'going, going, gone by mid-June.' Original plans called for the distribution of 750,000 MagiCans throughout the summer. I think approximately 200,000 cans were distributed before the promotion was ended early."

Moses pondered, "I could use this as an example of a breakdown in internal controls: both the quality control in manufacturing and the testing of consumer perception in marketing. Internal controls are used to ensure that each of the organization's activities are conducted properly. How did this affect your budget, since it's the principal means by which many financial controls are implemented?"

"Well, the performance reports were certainly off!" Chuck responded with a grin. "They compared the budgeted (expected) and reported (actual) performance at frequent intervals during the promotional campaign. As part of the initial planning process, the budget was developed to show how the organization would use its financial resources to achieve short-term objectives in the course of its operations over a defined time period. As a control device, the budget was successful. There are four elements of control, and the budget provided management with clear information for each element. The first element is determining which actions to perform. Secondly, controls are a preventive tool to assess whether ongoing operations are producing satisfactory performance. Third, controls provide feedback to determine whether changes are necessary to restore satisfactory performance. Were changes needed in the MagiCan promotion? Do chickens lay eggs? Anyway, the fourth element of control is comparison and follow-up. The optimal goal is to compare and determine when actual performance equals, or even surpasses, the performance projected in the budget! Needless to say, we didn't reach that optimal goal!"

"As I recall, Coke still managed to salvage its promotional campaign that summer. I remember drinking from Coke cups that had peel-off stickers with prizes underneath."

"Right. MagiCans were only part of the $100 million summer campaign, so we still had some tricks up our sleeve. You remember how big the vocal group, New Kids on the Block, was that summer. They were in commercials for Coca-Cola. At least we played it smart there and got celebrities that weren't controversial like Madonna."

Moses nodded, "I was glad when Pepsi pulled their commercials using Madonna. I thought her music video released about the same time was sacrilegious and offensive. I guess it was just bad timing for Pepsi that their promotions using Madonna coincided with the release of her music video. I'm sure they're more careful in selecting a spokesperson now. They wouldn't want to engender the wrath of consumers again!"

"The Coca-Cola Company executives still feel that technology is a great marketing tool in the soft-drink industry and that MagiCans still have potential. The company had double-digit sales gains during the first three weeks of MagiCan promotion. Hopefully, by pulling the promotion early, the image of the MagiCan wasn't overly damaged so that it'll be possible to relaunch an improved version later. Some marketing experts have even praised the company for their openness and quickness in dealing with the MagiCan defects. Some big corporations aren't so quick to own up to a mistake."

"Yes, I remember Perrier was guilty of that back in 1990. Some bottles of Perrier drinking water were found to be contaminated. Perrier was criticized for not quickly informing their consumers."

Chuck smiled, "I recall one story about the MagiCans that certainly wasn't funny at the time, but I can joke about it now. On a United Airlines flight, one of the attendants popped open a can of Coca-Cola Classic and nothing came out. By the weight of the can, she could tell that something was in there so she immediately became suspicious. A bomb squad was requested to meet the plane when it landed in San Francisco. Upon landing, the passengers were rushed off and the Coca-Cola can was taken to a remote area. The bomb squad carefully opened the can and found a $10 bill!"

* * *

"May I speak to Mr. Jones, please?" Moses asked.

"Sure. Take your choice," the voice replied, too jauntily for Moses's taste. "You want a Mr. Jones who's drawing Social Security, a Mr. Jones who is currently imbibing a large iced tea--that's me--or a Mr. Jones who's drawing flies while he's trying to get a tan in the back yard? That's my little brother."

"Uh, Mr. John Wayne Jones. From Wharton."

"You got him. What can I do for you?"

"This is Moses McDonald. I was on the faculty at Wharton until recently. Dr. Wilson suggested I get in touch with you about a consulting job that I'm involved in here in Atlanta."

"Billy! How's he doing? Did he ever get his office straightened out after setting fire to the wastebasket with his pipe? Funniest thing I've seen since a cat dropped a litter in Mrs. Reyher's basket of clean laundry, right on top of her stack of step-ins."

"Yes, he's got everything back into shape again. Not much damage, except to the wastebasket and a few books." Moses, normally not one to make snap judgments, made an exception in this case. He decided he liked neither this impudent young man nor the prospect of working with him. He was on the verge of terminating the conversation when two thoughts, tumbling over each other for acknowledgment, stopped him. First was the memory of Billy Wilson's enthusiastic recommendation of Jones. "The absolute best at wringing dirty laundry out of a computer," Wilson had said. The second was the recollection that Mike had placed him on a short lease, time-wise. The likelihood of finding anybody truly qualified in so short amount of time was slim, especially considering the nature of the job.

"Look, Mr. Jones, I know ..."

"Call me Duke, please," Jones interrupted. "My folks didn't have any children they gave the first name of 'Mr.' to."

"I know this is short notice," Moses continued, unable to bring himself to be so familiar as to use a nickname. "But I wonder if you could possibly drop by my office in Sandy Springs this evening about 5:30? I'd like to talk to you about the job I'm on. It shouldn't take but half an hour or so, and I'll be happy to pay your regular consultation fee."

"Sure. Just give me the address. I'm just a little south of the loop, so it won't take me long to get there."

* * *

Moses was just opening the door to the office when he was startled by a motorcycle careening into the driveway. Moses did not ride motorcycles. He did not like motorcycles, viewing them with the same distaste that he had for hot rods, dune buggies, and the many other diverse manifestations of the inexplicable compulsion some people have to turn perfectly reasonable vehicles of transport into weird, uncomfortable, unsightly, and frequently noisy contraptions. He instantly disliked this motorcycle more than most, since it sported an extended fork that tilted the bike so much it seemed someone had tried to turn the motorcycle into a mobile isosceles triangle. The rider astride the motorcycle seemed to have legs even longer than the fork that stretched interminably in front of the handlebars. He virtually undulated off the motorcycle and removed his helmet, revealing a shock of straight black hair as thick as a brand-new mop.

"Moses McDonald? I'm Duke Jones." The hand that engulfed Moses's felt like it was broad enough to pick up a 55-gallon drum. The owner of the hand appeared to be approximately as tall as a moderate-sized New England lighthouse.

"Yes, I'm Dr. McDonald, of course. Glad to meet you." Moses mentally kicked himself as he extracted his hand from the wrap-around grip. He never used the "Dr" title. People who insisted on announcing their academic credentials right off irritated him. But so did this six-foot-eight apparition in front of him, and even without realizing it he wanted to put some distance between himself and Duke. "Come on in. I asked my secretary to make a pot of coffee before she left. Let's see if she did."

"I'll pass on the coffee, thanks. Never drink anything that looks like it's made of floorsweep, I say. But you go ahead."

"I will, thank you. Why don't you grab a chair, and I'll be right with you." Moses thought grimly, "I am not going to be a very happy camper for the next few days." With resignation, he put aside his distaste, and began briefing Duke on the situation, leaving out any details on the office in-fighting and any references to Mike's moral lapses. Duke sat quietly, listening intently as he unconsciously pulled at a forelock of long black hair. Moses was surprised, when he got to the scam Brown had been pulling, at how quickly Duke caught on. In fact, he had interrupted to ask if the expense accounts had been checked even before Moses got around to telling him exactly what the scam had been. Then he had virtually barraged Moses with questions about the division's computer security, methods of access, and so on, till finally Moses had to call a halt. He was astonished to discover, on checking his watch, that almost three hours had passed.

This giant may be an odd duck, but he's no quack. He felt a bit more comfortable as he watched the lanky rider roar off, now officially associated with the consulting job for Coca-Cola.

Chapter 5

No matter when or how you close, remember that when you ask for the order it is very important to be silent. Do not say a single word. If you say something -- anything -- you increase your probability of losing the sale.

Charles M. Futrell

Moses had made arrangements to meet Duke at the Coca-Cola offices at ten o'clock the next morning. After a late start getting Katie off to school, he dropped into his own office to see how things were going, and picked up his briefcase. There he found his secretary, Doris, immersed in the intricacies of learning the new computer system. She seemed to have things well in hand. There had been no telephone calls. The world of corporate Atlanta was taking its time in beating a path to his door, as he had resigned himself to expect. Following a brief conversation with Doris, he left for his meeting with Duke.

Moses was always amused when he drove into the Coke complex. It seemed like a top secret military installation. There was a gate with a guard. No one could enter the premises without a name tag. In order for someone to visit, the guard had to call someone inside who gave permission for the person to enter. Moses parked in the visitor's parking lot and went into the building. His red name tag shone prominently on his coat lapel. He stopped at a Coke machine on the ground floor and got a free Diet Coke from the machine. Was it taxable? Oh, well, the Internal Revenue Service was probably not that picky.

As Moses drank his Diet Coke, he was amazed that something with so few calories could taste this good. Coca-Cola thought this new diet drink tasted so good that it was the first-ever line extension of the Coke trademark. That was back in 1982 and since then it's been the nation's leading diet soft drink. Diet Coke has accounted for the lion's share of Coke's domestic volume growth for several years.

One thing Moses enjoyed about his consulting jobs was picking up interesting information on the companies. He often used the information in his lectures. Diet Coke was a good example of using target marketing successfully. Coca-Cola took advantage of the market's fastest growing soft drink segment -- diet drinks. Diet drinkers met the four requirements for effective market segmentation: 1) the size and purchasing power of the segment could be measured; 2) the segment was large enough to be profitable; 3) Coke could reach and serve the segment; and 4) Coke was able to develop programs to attract the segment. Market surveys showed that the public felt they were sacrificing taste to save calories. Coke felt their drink tasted good enough to be positioned on taste rather than low calories. Thus, the theme "just for the taste of it" came about.

Coca-Cola followed all the proper steps in targeting their consumer market. First, they divided the soft drink market into segments according to behavior, specifically, the benefit sought in a soft drink. Coke saw a need for low calories with good taste. Another behavioral aspect that Coke understood was user status segment -- such as potential users, ex-users, first-time users, non-users, and regular users. Being a professor, Moses couldn't help but mentally list the other bases for market segmentation -- geographic, demographic, and psycho graphic (i.e., social class, life style, or personality). Since Coca-Cola has more than one market segment they target for their products, they use differentiated marketing (separate promotions for each segment) as opposed to undifferentiated marketing or concentrated marketing.

Coca-Cola did an excellent job in selecting the competitive position for Diet Coke; in other words, its market positioning. A product's position in the market is the place it occupies in consumers' minds relative to competing products. Diet Coke's position was based on its good taste attribute and its low calorie benefit. Coke attributes its diet drink success to a tasty formula, the venerable Coca-Cola trademark (i.e., reputation), and strong marketing.

In the lobby of the Coke complex were various displays of Coca-Cola memorabilia, promotional advertisements, and other promotional merchandise. There was a Russell Yo-Yo made in the Philippines, a pictorial evolution of the Coke can, a 1929 cold-box, a chronology of bottles used between 1900 and 1956, an 1891 Coca-Cola calendar, a syrup urn used as a premium in the 1890's, and more. The displays reminded him of a family vacation trip he had made long ago as a kid.

During one summer vacation, Moses' family traveled to Vicksburg, Mississippi to see its historical attractions, including the Biedenharn Candy Company and Museum of Coca Cola Memorabilia. The museum was located in downtown Vicksburg on Washington Street. Coca Cola was first bottled in 1894 in the restored building. The museum also featured Coca Cola memorabilia, a 1900 soda fountain, and an 1890 candy store. One of his best memories of the museum, however, was not an historical artifact, but the delicious ice cream float and homemade candy that provided immense refreshment on a hot Mississippi summer day.

Moses's parents enjoyed historical attractions. His father was particularly fond of old battlefields. The Vicksburg National Military Park was renowned as one of the best. The 16-mile driving tour of the old battlefield was etched in his mind, even after all the intervening years. He remembered reading how two Missouri units, one Confederate and one Union, directly opposed one another at a strategic location. In bloody battle, friend met friend and brother met brother.

As Moses walked into his office, something about it seemed different. The office wasn't as cheerful looking. Then he realized what it was, the big plant next to his desk was wilted and dead. Moses thought that was strange since the plant had been green and healthy yesterday. "Maybe I watered it too much," Moses mused.

Later that morning, at precisely ten o'clock, Moses was closeted with Chuck and Duke. Chuck covered essentially the same ground Moses had covered the night before, but not before exchanging a questioning glance at his old friend. Moses simply shrugged slightly and raised his eyebrows a tad to show his own perplexity. After all, how do you explain a Ph.D. candidate and alleged computer expert who shows up for work toting a motorcycle helmet with a ninja warrior emblazoned across the back and wearing an Hawaiian flowered shirt that seemed to scream its colors. When Chuck turned Moses and Duke over to his assistant, Linda Barfoot, Moses could almost see the second thoughts bumping against each other in Chuck's mind. They were no more numerous than his own.

"Tell me about your computer system. With so many subsidiaries in so many countries, how do you get the financial information to corporate headquarters?" Duke asked abruptly.

"We don't compile the data at remote locations and send it by mail like some companies," Linda responded.

"I assume you are talking about Pepsi."

"Sh-h-h-h," whispered Linda, with her index finger at her mouth. "Don't mention the P-word in here." She laughed.

"Actually some time ago we replaced the time-sharing, mainframe processing with personal computers at each location, with an international data network."

"The local person translates their local currency data, such as pounds, into U.S. dollars. They then report this data in both local currency and U.S. dollars, in similar format to be reviewed by headquarters personnel. More about foreign currency translation can be found on the Web (http://acct.tamu.edu/Smith/fctrans.htm). They--the local office--lock the data so that it can not be changed at a future date and then send it over a telecommunication network to headquarters. The main office can pull each location's financial information into its PC network."

"What security procedures do you employ?" Duke asked.

"Hopefully a good, safe system." Linda replied with a grin. "We have designated microcomputer rooms, security stations with steel doors, passwords..."

"Passwords are notoriously ineffective as an access-control technique," Duke interrupted.

"We have a user identity code and automatic password obsolescence on a short-time cycle basis. Further, to use the computer, the valid user must be at a valid terminal on a valid day of the week. To stop an unauthorized person from accessing the computer while the approved person is also using the system, the computer checks and will disconnect both users. We believe that securing the mainframe is not enough. More computer processing power is in the network of PCs on our employees' desks than at the data center."

"Do you have TEMPESTs on your PCs?"

"Not yet. You are referring to the prevention of our PCs from radiating electromagnetic signals. We don't have any sensitive, classified governmental information in our system. The Coke and Diet Coke formulas are locked in a bank vault at Trust Company of Georgia. Only a handful of people know the formulas."

"How about using cryptographic technology to protect your communication signals?"

"No. Again, we are not like NASA or the CIA."

"What about separation of duties?"

"Data input and data output analysis are performed by different people. Library file procedures, programming, and actual system use are done by different people. We try to stop the fraud from occurring, but if fraud does occur, we can probably detect it."

Moses had to admit to himself, as Duke put a particularly pointed question to Linda, "This guy knows what he's talking about. At least Billy wasn't wrong about his technical expertise. I wonder if he's ever seen that ridiculous motorcycle, though."

Linda continued her discussion for fifteen minutes, and then Duke was left to check the computer system. He checked the logs of the unsuccessful sign-on attempts and the unsuccessful access attempts. Duke did not finish his review of the security controls until noon.

He made a note to check Coke's contingency plans for a fire in the data processing center. Were most of the computer software stored in off-site fireproof safes? He knew that three out of four businesses hit by fire could not survive the ninety days necessary to rebuild a destroyed computer system. He had read of the fire that destroyed Worlco, Inc., a twenty-five million dollar insurance and health care business. Due to planning, this company was able to resume collection and payments clerically and by a computer in a service bureau in a nearby city. What if a bursting pipe flooded the computer center?

Suppose a disgruntled employee reformatted the hard disks?

Duke searched out Linda to ask her the questions he had noted. "So ... how about we talk over lunch?"

Linda brushed back a lock of dark red hair and glanced up from the terminal. Duke was looming over her right elbow, holding a sheaf of papers.

"What's that?" she asked.

"The standardized immatrization synchronization for the primary syncolathe during the past quarter," Duke replied.

"What?" Linda reached for the papers and quickly rifled through them. "What is this? A laundry bill. A book report. A magazine. This is a ... what did you call it?"

"The quarterly standardized immatrization synchronization for the primary syncolathe, or something like that. But you can call it anything you wish. Call it an old laundry bill. Call it a dog-eared copy of *Advertising Age*. What I'd rather do is call it an invitation to lunch. How about it?"

"Uh...sounds fine. Give me a minute to write this onto the disk and pop by the ladies room. Just one question: Do we have to discuss how you starch your shirts? Or can we confine it to the scientific procedure used in looking for rainbows?"

"We can talk about whatever you wish, dear lady, though I'd prefer to spend my time talking only about you."

"Short conversation. Be back in a second."

* * *

"You're kidding. You jest. You can't be serious. That's what we're going to lunch in?" Linda looked with dismay at the motorcycle.

"Sure," Duke replied.

"You really expect me to go to lunch on something out of a motorcycle gang flick? I can't do that."

"Sure you can. You're wearing slacks. I brought an extra helmet today, just for you. You'll like it. Naturally air-conditioned.

Specially designed to make you feel you're a part of your environment. The ambiance of transportation at its absolute best. You'll get a lot of utility from it!"

"Utility?" questioned Linda.

"Yea, that ole economic term which refers to the satisfaction you'll receive from using, or consuming, a product; especially motorcycles. I'll admit, the motorcycle doesn't totally satisfy me. I'd need a Porsche for that. Since I'm currently funding my education though, I had to settle for utility maximization using the limited financial resources available."

"You've got to stop throwing out these economic terms. I don't have a textbook on me!"

"I'm just trying to impress you with my large brain size! There are some doorways that I can't fit through! Economics lesson two; utility maximization is the way a consumer adjusts consumption, given a budget constraint and a set of prices, in order to maximize the total amount of satisfaction. Stick with me, kid, and you'll go far!"

"You're impossible, Duke," Linda laughed. "Okay, I'll ride with you. But get out of here quick, will you, before somebody sees me. Please, don't try any loops or rolls, and take it slow. I value every single part of my anatomy just like it is. I don't want anything rearranged by somebody's bumper."

"A sentiment about your anatomy that I share completely," Duke said as he buckled on her helmet. In a few minutes they were approaching the dining establishment.

"The Varsity," Linda said. "Now that's a switch for a luncheon date. I haven't been here in ages, since I dated a Georgia Tech student years ago."

"We could try someplace else," Duke said, though not with much enthusiasm.

"Oh, no, it's perfect," Linda responded quickly. "Nothing would go better with a Harley than a Varsity hot dog. We will eat inside, though. I'm putting my foot down on that. Besides, there's no place to hang a tray on this contraption."

"Whatever you say, m'lady. It does seem to me, though, that if you're going to be dining at the world's largest drive-in, you ought to be willing to experience it fully."

"I'm going to experience it fully from inside. And, I suspect my co-workers will experience a bit of it, too, when I get back to the office, because I'm going to get onion rings along with my hot dog."

After they'd received their hot dogs and drinks, Linda asked, "Is Duke your real name or a nickname?"

"My parents were big fans of John Wayne; that's my real name, John Wayne Jones. Of course that carries with it the nickname of Duke. What's your full name?"

"Linda Lou Barfoot."

"Linda Lou," Duke said pensively. "I like it! That's what I'm going to call you."

"Tell me about yourself, Linda Lou. Are you from here? Where did you go to school? How long have you been with Coke? Do you dye your eyes, or are they that color naturally? Can we do this tomorrow? Can we do it the day after tomorrow? When can I get you to pose for someone to paint your picture on your helmet?"

"Whoa, easy rider. One at a time, please. Yes, I'm from around here, sort of. I grew up in Savannah. My dad died during my senior year in high school. Money was very tight after Dad's death. Mom managed to hang on until I graduated, but then we moved up here so I could go to school at Georgia State and she could go to work at my uncle's business. He runs an auto parts store in Smyrna, and Mom is his office manager."

"I'm sorry about your dad. Both my parents are still alive. I'm thankful that they're both in good health."

Linda looked off into the distance. "Sometimes I really miss him. Have you ever heard that oldie-goldie tune, 'Everything I own,' by the 1970s music group Bread. The lyrics go 'I would give everything I own just to have you back again.' Most people assume that the song was about a lost love, but actually it was a tribute to the songwriter's deceased father. Well, that's how I feel about my dad."

Linda looked back toward Duke who had assumed a rather solemn expression. She smiled at him. "Hey, cheer up. Life goes on.

With God's help, I've made it. I'm just thankful for the 17 years that I had a father. I have some wonderful memories. Some of my friends never really knew a dad, even though their dad's are still alive. You know the type, workaholics."

"Yeah. I've never understood people who valued their jobs more than their families or friends."

"What about your parents?" Linda asked.

"Well, they're celebrating their fortieth wedding anniversary next month. Mom teaches high school typing and Pop's an economics professor at a state university. Pop's quite a character. He thought he was through with school after finishing the seventh grade. He had to go to work. He grew up in a very rural area. Pop worked as a farmer, as a roughneck on offshore oil drilling rigs, as a logger, and as a tire factory worker. When he turned 20, he was drafted for the Korean War. As he tells the story, his being drafted is what ended the war."

"How's that?" Linda queried.

"Pop says that the communists were too scared to keep fighting when they heard that he was coming." Duke grinned.

"Very funny," Linda responded, "but how did he wind up as a college professor?"

"To make a long story short, my pop passed the high school equivalency test and entered college. He went all the way through the Ph.D. He said one thing that really motivated him was the professor who counseled him during his first college semester. The professor told him that some people were college material and some weren't, and that my pop was in the latter category. Pop set out to prove that professor wrong."

"I would say he did," Linda interjected.

"I reckon I've talked an earful. Tell me more about you. You said you went to Georgia State. I hear that Coke contributes a lot of money to Emory University."

"I went to State full-time for two and a half years. I couldn't afford Emory. My college fund ran out and I had to go to work full time. I worked in sales for four years and finished my degree at night school, with a major in marketing and a minor in computer science.

Then I came to Coke."

"As you know, Chuck Morgan is my supervisor. I work in the marketing services area for the overseas development division. My job is very challenging and interesting. I'm involved with Coca-Cola's media coverage, packaging, vending services, and sales promotions. That gives me input into two areas of the marketing communications mix -- sales promotion and public relations. Sales promotions really stretch our creativity, since it involves all short-term incentives to encourage sales. We're not big on coupons, but I can't even remember all the different contests we've had. Through our sales promos, we've been successful in achieving other objectives besides increasing sales, such as increasing market share, encouraging brand switching, getting dealers to push our products, and motivating our salesforce."

"One really great advantage of working for a large company like Coca-Cola is that my department is usually budgeted the monetary resources needed to achieve our objectives. Through the objective-and-task method of budgeting, we define objectives, determine the tasks that must then be performed to achieve these objectives, and estimate the costs of the tasks. Some of the product lines have a percentage-of-sales budgeting method. For marketing, our approach is heaven compared to the firms which use the affordable method, spend only what the firm thinks it can afford! I think some of our competitors use the competitive-parity method, which bases the promotion budget on what a competitor spends."

Linda smiled briefly and continued. "My computer know-how has been invaluable in my job. I do all my analysis on the computer, along with spreadsheets and research data. Enough about my work; I get carried away once I start."

She paused for a moment and then looked into Duke's eyes. "To answer your other questions, the eyes are my own, all the way. And I don't know about tomorrow, or the day after, or next year. But if we do do this again, I'll tell you right now we won't be moseying out on that piece of motorized mayhem you own. I don't exactly trust the driving skills of a guy whose helmet and jacket feature a ninja warrior. Meanwhile, you'd better finish that second hot dog so we can get back to the office. I want to be off that motorcycle before the rest of the crew starts returning from what I suspect was a far saner lunch hour than we had."

Her smile, Duke decided, showed she didn't mean a word of it. "I'm getting a lot of marginal utility from this second hot dog!"

Linda laughed, "Here we go again! OK, I'll bite: pun intended!"

Duke was enjoying Linda's sense of humor, and the opportunity to show off a little. "Marginal utility is the amount of utility added by an additional unit of consumption."

"Two can play this game," Linda said with a sly grin. "My marginal utility is diminishing as I eat the last of my onion rings!"

"Either you catch on real quick, or you've been holding out on me! Just so I'm not out-done, diminishing marginal utility is the fact that marginal utility declines as consumption increases."

Linda joined in, "To put it in layman's terms, the more onion rings I consume, the less satisfaction I get from each additional deep-fried ring of fat!"

Later that night Duke thought about Linda Lou. She had those eyes that were so hard to explain, like intangible assets. They were special, but not because they were so beautifully blue. They had those sparkles that tell you that she has a special interest in you. Yes, they were beautiful, but Linda Lou's eyes were more. Her piercing gaze revealed a sharp mind working behind those eyes. She was attractive, intelligent, caring, and resourceful. She was competing in a man's world which had been slow in opening its managerial doors and executive suites to women. Duke felt a suspicion growing that he was in for some novel learning experiences with Linda Lou -- assuming that she was interested in him at all. Duke realized he was scowling at himself, and wondered why.

Chapter 6

Coca-Cola is militant about protecting its brand name and has successfully sued over 800 retailers for serving another brand when a customer orders "a Coke."

John Koten

On their second date, Linda picked up Duke in her American made sports car. The two of them had agreed to go ice-skating.

"Maybe I'm not supposed to ask this, but I'm going to anyway." The words were spoken lightly, as Linda tilted her head slightly to the left. The mannerism was one of the first things Duke had noticed about her. Never to the right, and never more than a little off the vertical. He found it charming. He was definitely enjoying their date.

"Ask, me anything, Linda Lou," Duke replied. "Can I make ice cream sodas the old fashioned way, sodas that would lure a leopard out of a tree? Do I sleep in socks? Does baldness run in my family? Are fatigues really my favorite apparel? Are most Mensa members egocentric insecure bores? Is there life after 30? Do I want to take you on a romantic cruise to the South Seas and live on coconuts and palm juice while the Polynesian breezes play harmony for the melodies my heart sings when I am near you? The answer is yes, and yes, and yes again."

Linda smiled, "The answer to all of the foregoing questions is that you can be the most exasperating, irreverent ball of blarney I've ever encountered."

"Ah ... You've found my one weakness. Flattery. Give me more."

"What are you and Dr. McDonald doing at the office? I know it's something out of the ordinary. You're in the office all day long, and it's been a couple of weeks now. What's going on? Has somebody been embezzling money, or something like that? Everybody in the office is curious. First Chris Brown submits his resignation without any notice. And now his wife's been transferred over to another division."

"It's the Grinch," Duke replied.

"The what?"

"The Grinch," Duke repeated. "The Grinch that stole Christmas. He's stashed it in a Coca-Cola warehouse somewhere, and we're trying to smoke it out. So far, all we've turned up is a couple of missing Easters and one lost Ground Hog Day. But we're getting close. Just yesterday Moses caught the scent of eggnog emanating out of a warehouse in Spokane. Turned out to be a conventioneer from Waco, Texas, though, who'd gone out there last New Year's and had such a good time he didn't make it back home on time. Now he's afraid to go home; his wife, it seems, is a butcher. Wields a mean cleaver."

"Be serious, Duke."

"Okay. Look, all we're doing is taking a look to see how secure the computer system is. It's no big thing. Somebody should have done it long ago."

"How secure? How secure does it need to be? Heavens to Betsy! Coca-Cola isn't the Defense Department, even though we may like to think we're more important than the government. Somebody is going to steal classified Coca-Cola information, like how many days vacation a Clerk III has accrued? That's ridiculous."

"Not really," Duke responded. The jocularity was gone. "A competitor would love to have all of your marketing and sales data. Besides, every record on that computer represents time, if nothing else. Lose them, through negligence or malice, and it would cost Coke a nice sum to compile them again. And that's assuming all of them could be reconstituted. Some of that data is stored only in the computer."

"You're right, I'm sure," Linda said. "I just got the impression it was more than that, that perhaps something was wrong."

"I think your job's safe," Duke said teasingly. "That is, unless you've got a garage full of purloined Christmas presents. Is that a strand of tinsel I detect deep in your auburn tresses?"

"That, I'm sure, is one of the many strands of gray hair I have acquired since I began spending too much time with a harebrained immigrant from some unknown planet," Linda replied, laughing. "The rink is right ahead. I'm going to warn you again. Pull any funny stuff out on the floor, and I'll cut you off at the knees. Ice-skating is not the best idea you've had. I prefer my transportation device to come with an automatic transmission and velour seats."

"You have indeed shown admirable taste in that department," Duke said as he patted the Dodge Stealth's upholstery. "But I still think we should have come on Pegasus."

"No way, Jose," Linda said firmly. "If I have to take a trip to the hospital emergency room, I'm not going to do it on the back of a motorcycle. That's final."

* * *

Chuck Morgan looked downcast, like a kid who'd just found out his favorite Saturday morning cartoon had been canceled. He looked at Moses almost as if he was pleading.

"Are you sure? Ernie Anbert is one of our best people. He's been our division employee of the month twice. He's never taken a single sick day. We have to force him to take vacations. He goes to my church. Heck, my daughter's even gone out with him a couple of times when she's been home from college. We've got to know what we're talking about on this one."

"I don't think there's any doubt," Duke Jones interjected quietly, but with a conviction Moses found compelling. Duke gestured with his left hand, flashing the Ace bandage that he'd shown up wearing that morning. The computer whiz had mumbled something about a skating accident when Moses had inquired. Duke hadn't volunteered more, and Moses hadn't pursued the matter because his associate was obviously a bit chagrined about the injury. Probably something to do with that attractive young woman Duke had been squiring around, Moses thought wryly. The course of young love obviously had a few unexpected and painful turns.

"We've tracked it back now for six months, and cross-referenced it to every operator who's worked here during that time," Duke was continuing. "It's Anbert, all right. Or at least part of the problem is. Here, let me show you."

With a start, Moses realized he was relieved to let Duke take the lead in the conference. Moses was nothing if not perceptive. The esteem in which Anbert was held by senior and junior staffers alike had not escaped him, and he had not looked forward to laying out the facts for Chuck. But that was part of his job, and he had long ago learned to distance himself from it.

No, this was something else. Where his profession was concerned, Moses let no one in front of him unless the person had earned it. It came as a surprise to discover that the rambunctious, irreverent, outrageous John Wayne "Duke" Jones, over the past two weeks, had somehow sneaked up on the blind side of Moses' respect. With a smile and a new perspective, he relaxed and watched Duke at work.

"Like I say, we went back six months," Duke was saying. "We charted the shift of every operator you have in the division. Then we charted the time periods when we know, beyond any doubt, that you had lost computer time. We were able to verify that time had been lost by comparing the logs and repetitive programs that require essentially the same amount of time each time they are run. We found one operator who was on duty on each occasion that you lost computer time. The operator was Ernie Anbert."

"Is there any other explanation?" Chuck asked. The resignation in his voice was almost tangible.

"No," Duke replied. "I wish there was, but there isn't."

"Well, I guess that's that, then. Get it all lined up, and we'll have him in after lunch."

"There's one other thing," Duke said. Moses sat up expectantly. Duke had not mentioned to him anything other than the same information he'd already given Chuck. "He either doesn't care if he's caught, or he wants to be identified. One of these unauthorized usage times was just last week, after he knew about our investigation."

"I'll have him in at 2 o'clock," Chuck said. "I'll want both of you here when I confront him."

* * *

"Yes sir," Ernie Anbert said as he strode into Chuck's office. "Linda said you wanted to see me." The words were hardly uttered before the employee caught sight of Moses and Duke, seated on the sofa across from Chuck's desk. Moses watched closely. He saw no visible evidence that the presence of the two auditors caused Ernie any consternation.

"Sit down, Ernie," Chuck replied. "There's a problem we need to discuss with you. You've met Moses McDonald and Mr. Jones, I believe?" Moses smiled inwardly: it was "Moses McDonald," but "Mr. Jones." Looks like the buttoned-down corporation mind-set has taken root with my old friend, he thought. He can't bring himself in a business conference to use a nickname like Duke.

"Yes, I've been talking with both of them for about a week now," Ernie responded. "What's the problem?" This time, Moses noted, there was a hint of apprehension in the youngster's voice.

"It seems there has been some unauthorized use of the computer," Chuck said sternly. "It has been traced to you, as late as last week. That's pretty serious, Ernie. It can mean termination. Want to tell me about it?"

Watching Ernie's face was like watching a Christmas sparkler fade and die. The brightness ebbed, and nothing but the dry ash of despair remained. The long silence that ensued was broken only by the creak of the sofa as Duke shifted his weight.

Finally, Ernie straightened and said in a voice low but resolute. "You're right, Mr. Morgan. I have been using the system, for about two years now. Not very much, never more than 10 minutes at a time. I'm sorry I did, and it was a stupid thing to do. But I did, and I'll own up to it whether you've got any evidence of it or not."

"How about telling us about it?"

"There's nothing much to tell." Ernie was regaining control, and the confidence had returned to his voice.

I like this kid, Moses thought. It's a shame he had to pull something like this. Let's hope he hasn't been up to some real dirty tricks.

"About two years ago, I purchased some software for a baseball card inventory and value system. That's what I've been doing, updating my baseball card inventory. I only do it on my breaks. That's all."

"That's all! What do you mean, 'That's all' ?'" Chuck said with great agitation. "Don't you know that's a cardinal rule around here! Never bring in any outside programming? My goodness, son, surely you realize what could happen to our system if a virus ever got into it?"

"I know it's against company policy, Mr. Morgan. " Ernie was contrite, but his demeanor was far from hang-dog. He was pleading his case, and doing a pretty good job, Moses thought. "But I want you to understand. My system at home is secure. Nothing has ever gone into it that didn't come still wrapped in cellophane from the manufacturer. I used brand-new disks to copy the software onto, and that's what I uploaded to our system. I know it doesn't mean anything to you, but I wouldn't even download anything from Coke's computer into mine. Once I worked out the inventory on our system, I went home and duplicated it on mine. I'm sure my system is free of any viruses; I'm not sure about the company's."

"I know computer viruses are very dangerous. There's almost no way to detect the presence of a new virus. Once it gets into a system some way -- by being programmed in, or by having it downloaded from somewhere else, you often can't detect it. I know what damage they can do. There's a lot about computer viruses on the Web (http://acct.tamu.edu/smith/virus.htm). A virus can wipe out every bit of programming. They're malevolent, and anybody who'd infect a system with a virus has got to be sick. Anybody who would permit one to get into a system is inexcusably negligent. I know that. I may have been stupid in breaking a company rule, but our system hasn't been compromised because of me. I'll take my licks--I know I've got 'em coming -- but you've got greater security problems to worry about."

"What do you mean?" Chuck demanded. All three men were immediately alert, intent on what Ernie was saying.

"Come on and I'll show you," Ernie said, rising.

Just as Ernie finished speaking, the phone rang. Chuck answered and after a moment said, "Moses, go check this out. I need to handle this call." Ernie Anbert led Moses and Duke to the information systems department.

Walking down the hall Moses asked, "Aren't you a little old to collect baseball cards?"

Ernie's eyes lit up. "Baseball cards are an impressive investment. An academic analysis by a Professor Krause in the late eighties showed that rookie baseball cards were the top investments of the 1980's."

"Baseball cards?" Duke questioned in disbelief.

"Absolutely. A T206 Honus Wagner card from a 1909-11 set, with a crease, sold for $110,000. Fewer than 100 of these cards are known to be in existence. The Goudey Gum Company 240-card collection from 1933--including Babe Ruth and Lou Gehrig--sells for about $18,000."

Moses said, "My mother threw away all of my baseball cards and comic books many years ago."

"That's probably why the old baseball cards are so valuable," Ernie replied. "Did you have any DC *Detective Comics*? A complete mint run of *Detective Comics* retails for about $150,000. Over the past five year period the average yearly return has been 36%."

"Holy Bat Caves," Moses said mockingly. "I used to read Batman and Superman comics. My daughter, however, prefers Wonder Woman."

Ernie continued, "Of course, it's hard to find high-quality investment comics. The acid left in comic book paper during the manufacturing process is the major cause of aging and yellowing."

"I suppose some salesmen received their first training by trading baseball cards. Why do you need a computer inventory?" asked Duke.

"So many cards," answered Ernie. "A complete annual set of every player who goes to spring training camps contains at least 750 cards, costing about $20."

Moses laughed and said," Next you'll tell me you sold short

Pete Rose cards when they investigated him for gambling, and later went to prison."

"Hey, don't laugh. There are even counterfeit Pete Rose cards. My Mark McGuire card really went up in value in 1998 when he hit 70 home runs and broke Roger Maris' long-standing record of 61. Let me tell you about the most infamous baseball card ever issued--the 1989 Fleer Bill Pipken card. Number 616."

Ernie lowered his voice, "It's the Jesse James of baseball cards. Bill Pipken, a so-so second baseman, posed with a profanity printed on the knob of his bat. After Fleer wiped the egg off their face, they recalled the offensive card."

When they arrived at the information systems department, Ernie sat down at his computer workstation. The workstation was an IBM microcomputer hardwired to the Coke network. In other words, Ernie could run any number of applications at his microcomputer or tie into the network for network applications such as searching various corporate databases.

Moses noticed a book, *Standard Catalog of Baseball Cards*, on Ernie's desk. He picked up and flipped through a softback book entitled *How to Collect Baseball Cards*, by Krause and Crumbley. He noticed a Pepper and Salt cartoon from the *Wall Street Journal* apparently used as a book marker. It showed a loan officer pointing to a small boy. The caption stated: "This is Scotty. He has to approve all loans for which baseball cards are offered for collateral."

Ernie motioned for Moses and Duke to take a seat. Ernie swallowed hard and then said, "Heck, I didn't think updating my inventory occasionally would raise any eyebrows when the higher-ups were using the computer a hundred times more often for their unofficial jobs. Just look at this." At that, Ernie's fingers began flying over the keyboard.

After logging in his user-ID, ANBERT, and password, SESAME, Ernie retrieved the mainframe's computer log and displayed it on his microcomputer's monitor screen. The log listed all the jobs run on the Coke network server computer for the past 30 days. He pointed to some line items here and there as he scrolled through the log. He said as he pointed, "You can see my inventory and pricing activities appeared in the log as 'log time' and caused interruptions between the processing of other programs. Of course you already know this. That's how you fingered me, isn't it?"

"Get to your point," Duke said, getting rather bored looking at the computer log.

"Yes, get to your point," Moses added, "You said you had something to show us." Moses removed his photo-tinted grey glasses in order to see better. They were camouflaged bifocals.

"Well, before I do, I want to know what's in it for me. I don't like squealing on a fellow computer jock, but I just want you to know my fooling around is really insignificant compared to other people's unofficial use of the machine."

"What makes you think you have something we don't already know?" Duke replied sharply.

"Maybe I don't, but how are you going to know if I don't tell you?" Ernie replied cautiously.

"Sure, if you have something really important, we won't make a big deal out of your baseball card inventory. Of course, you'll have to give us a piece of bubble-gum. But don't push us, Ernie. Remember, you're the one in trouble," Moses said with a frown.

"All right, then, look at this," Ernie pointed to the amber screen.

Moses and Duke looked. "I don't get it," Duke said. "That's where somebody ran the online query and search program. What's so unusual or revealing about that?"

"Nothing, if that was the only time, but look here and here." Ernie pointed to a score of similar listings as he continued scrolling down the screen. "The key thing," Ernie added as he scrolled and pointed, "is the user ID number. It's not on the registered ID list. It shouldn't work. This person shouldn't be able to do this. He didn't just come up with someone else's valid ID and associated password. He must have gotten in using a trap door. I haven't bothered to see when it started, but he's been doing this for at least a year. That's when I first noticed it, anyway. I didn't turn him in because I thought it might be one of my buddies in operations. Later I found out it wasn't."

Duke interjected, "Well, why didn't you at least bring it up then?"

"Why?" said Ernie, "I couldn't see any harm being done. Shoot, it might just be some kid out there hacking. I didn't want anyone to get in trouble over nothing. Besides, when I was in high school I used to hack and tried to break into every computer system I could -- just for the fun of it. I never hurt anything. It was just a game with me, as well as some of my friends."

"My point is that this system," continued Ernie, "has some real security problems. This illegal entry is just one example of what might be going on all over the system. This log only covers activities in the inventory section of the system, which is where I do most of my programming."

"And your baseball cards inventory," added Duke in a monotone. His face offered no hint of a smile.

"Right," said Ernie with a grimace.

"So what do you think?" continued Ernie.

"We'll let you know," replied Moses. "Duke, let's go up to my office and discuss this. Ernie, we'll get back to you tomorrow." At that, Moses and Duke got up and walked out the door, leaving Ernie with a solemn look on his face.

"So what do you think?" Moses asked Duke as they entered Moses's temporary workstation at the Coke office.

"Well, the baseball cards activity is harmless enough, but I can't understand why Ernie didn't inform the systems manager of this security problem. I'm going to check into it, but I have a feeling this problem is bigger than just some pimple-faced high school kid hacking. For one thing, a hacker would have been bored to death looking at inventory records long before a year was up."

"I get your point, Duke. What about this `trap door' thing? As I understand, that's a technique programmers use to get around controls, but exactly how do they do it?"

"It's no big deal, Moses. When a program is being written or changed, it's possible for a programmer to include some breaks--that is, trap doors -- in the program code, making it possible to insert additional instructions and to provide intermediate output capability. It's a handy tool for programmers trying to debug a system. Unfortunately, it also makes it possible to insert unauthorized program procedures. These unauthorized procedures facilitate abuse."

Moses looked puzzled and asked, "Give me an example."

Duke replied, "The best example of a trap door program is what is commonly referred to as a ZAP program. Programmers typically set up a utility ZAP program to modify other programs and data while bypassing controls. Don't get me wrong, a ZAP program can have legitimate uses. Most programmers wouldn't misuse a ZAP program, but the potential is there. The worst part is that the use of a ZAP program leaves few footprints. A 'Trojan Horse' program is another type of trap door. It involves hidden programming code within another program to provide unauthorized entry into a system. Someone appears to have used a 'Trojan Horse' in this case."

"So you think it was a Coke programmer who's been searching the files for who knows what," interrupted Moses.

"Probably. On the other hand, it could be an outside hacker, although it would take someone knowledgeable about both programming and the Coke computer system to pull it off. Perhaps a former Coke employee," Duke answered.

"Then it could be an inside job?" asked Moses.

"Well, yes, but let's not jump to conclusions. I have a few things to check out before I point any fingers. No one is beyond suspicion, even Ernie Anbert. This stunt could be something he's done in addition to his baseball card inventory."

"Wait a doggone minute, Duke. He's the one who told us about this, remember?"

"Hey, it's a possibility. He might figure we can't determine who the culprit is. Plus, it's a great smokescreen. We're not worried about his extracurricular activities keeping track of the prices of baseball cards anymore. Of course, you're right--he's not a likely possibility. My point is--you have to keep your eyes open and not rule anything out. Don't faint, but it could even be your old friend, Chuck

Morgan."

Moses's mouth dropped open, but before he could speak Duke slapped him on the back and said, "Just kidding."

"I'm glad. You just don't know what an honorable guy Chuck really is!" responded Moses, still taken aback at this lighthearted character assassination of his old friend and current employer.

"No offense, Moe, but just remember 'power corrupts and absolute power corrupts absolutely.'"

"I'll buy that as a general rule, but there are individuals in this world who hold honor above petty material gains," said Moses, feeling a little hostile toward Duke.

"Whoa, buddy, I can see I've touched a nerve. I guess I'm a little too cynical. I've seen too many upstanding people give in to temptation. It's just something about the computer that tempts some people to assume they can get away with anything. They think just because they do it on the computer, nobody will be able to trace their clandestine activities back to them."

"And that's a valid assumption if the audit trail gets lost in the computer system." Moses said, beginning to feel less angry toward Duke.

"Right, old chap. The problem with many computer systems is that security has not been carefully maintained. It's no wonder there's so much computer crime. The average computer crime has been estimated to cost $600,000. Why, the average white-collar crime is only $23,500, and the average armed robbery is even less, only $250. Five hundred grand is a pretty big temptation. What's more amazing is the chance of prosecution is almost nonexistent. Statistics show the bigger the dollar amount of a crime, the smaller its probability of prosecution."

"You must be kidding!"

"I wish I was. It certainly can make one cynical about justice in America." Moses sighed.

Moses looked at his Mickey Mouse watch and realized it was time to leave for his class at the university. Students don't wait very long before they decide the teacher isn't coming. "My daughter, Katie, is cooking something special tomorrow night. How about joining us?"

Duke smiled, "Sounds good. Amazingly, my busy single's calendar is open tomorrow!"

* * *

After racing across town, Moses found himself facing a room full of inquiring minds. He placed an overhead transparency on the projector. He pointed to the screen and said, "Price is a major influence on buyer choice. The price of a product or service cannot be set arbitrarily."

Pointing to the display screen, he explained, "Companies should consider internal factors when setting prices." The display screen showed the following:

Internal factors include:

1. Marketing objectives --
   For example, a goal of market-share leadership calls for low prices in order to increase sales. A goal of product quality leadership calls for high prices to support high quality and research.
2. Marketing mix --
   The price must be sufficient to cover costs of other items in the marketing mix; these are product design, distribution, and promotion. Costs plus a fair rate of return set the floor on prices.

After reading the internal factors, Moses switched transparencies. "There are three external factors which should be considered in setting prices. Moses pointed to the screen.

External factors include:

1. Market structure --
   This is dependent upon the product and the number of competitors.
2. Economic demand & supply
3. Government regulations

"Typically, when referring to economic demand, we want to know what happens when the price of a product changes relative to the prices of other products. We focus on price and assume all other factors which affect demand are unchanged. Other factors include consumer preferences, expectations, income, and prices of other products. These factors become the 'ceteris paribus' conditions. Ceteria paribus is a Latin term that means 'holding everything else constant.'"

"Consequently, we can state the law of demand as follows: The quantity demanded of a good or service is an inverse function of its price, ceteris paribus. In simple terms, this means that consumers will purchase more of a good or service at a lower price; and as price rises, consumers will demand a smaller quantity of the good."

"A demand schedule shows the quantity of a product which is demanded at various prices. This schedule can then be conformed to a graph to show the demand curve for the product."

"Economists spend a great amount of time distinguishing clearly between changes along a demand curve and changes (or shifts) of the curve itself. Changes along the curve represent 'changes in quantity demanded' caused solely by a change in the price of a good. Changes (or shifts) of the curve represent changes in demand resulting from changes in any of the ceteris paribus conditions."

"A supply schedule presents the quantity of goods offered for sale at a specific time and at a specific price. Four factors are typically associated with supply. They are the price of the good, the price of the factors of production, the level of technology, and expectations concerning the first three factors. We can state the law of supply as follows: The quantity supplied of a good or service is usually a positive function of price, ceteris paribus. This means that suppliers will usually supply less of an item at lower prices; and as prices rise, the quantity supplied will also increase."

"The distinction between supply and quantity supplied is very important, just as it is between demand and quantity demanded. Changes along the supply curve represent 'changes in quantity supplied' caused solely by changes in price. A change (or shift) of the curve represents a change in supply caused by changes in one or more of the ceteris paribus conditions."

"An important difference between the law of demand and the law of supply is the word 'usually.' This has led some economists to say that the law of supply is 'not quite' a law because of exceptions to the usual relationship between price and quantity supplied. An exception to the general rule occurs where there is no time to produce more units, such as stadium seats at a sold-out football game, or when a unique supplier no longer exists, such as sculptures by Rodin."

Near the back of the classroom, a student raised her hand. Moses turned his attention toward the student and asked, "A question?"

"Yes, Dr. McDonald. Could you explain the factors of production?"

"I would be glad to do so," Moses responded. "The factors of production are defined as the inputs of land, labor, capital, and entrepreneurship that a firm uses to produce outputs, that is, goods or services. For example, if the costs of these factors decrease, then supply should increase."

A student raised a question; "Isn't that part of former President Reagan's supply-side economics?"

"Yes. The idea is, if the business community sees the potential for costs to be lowered because of fewer government regulations, and the potential for greater profits through decreased taxes and faster depreciation, supply will increase."

"When we combine a market's supply curve and demand curve on a graph, the intersection of the two lines will give us market equilibrium. The equilibrium is the price and quantity that will exist in the market if no impediments are placed on the free working of the market."

"In setting prices, what we're especially interested in is the price elasticity of demand. Elasticity measures the way one variable changes in response to changes in other variables. Thus, the price elasticity of demand is a measure of the responsiveness of the quantity demanded to changes in price. For some products such as entertainment items or hamburgers, consumers will vary the amount they buy depending on what the price is. These products have a relatively *elastic* demand curve which is very responsive to changes in price. Other products, such as textbooks and designer clothes, will sell close to the same amount regardless of changes in price. These products have a relatively *inelastic* demand curve which is not very responsive to changes in price. The number of substitutes a product has is a major influence on its price elasticity of demand. There are lots of substitutes for hamburgers as a fast food item, such as pizza, hot dogs, or tacos."

"Some products have a varying elastic demand curve. Demand may not change very much (inelastic) as the price increases, until a certain price is reached and then demand becomes more responsive to price (elastic). For example, most consumers may continue buying their favorite shampoo until it reaches $6 a bottle. Then, with each additional price increase, more and more consumers quit buying."

"In determining price, which will affect the quantity demanded, the goal is to increase total revenue of course." Moses pointed to a student on the back row. "Mr. Seymour, remind us of what the total revenue equation is."

"The quantity sold multiplied by the price of the product."

"Thank you. A price change has two effects on total revenue, and they are opposite. A price decrease, given the same quantity demanded, will decrease total revenue. However, that same price decrease will usually cause the quantity demanded to increase which has a positive effect on total revenue. The key question is whether the percentage increase in quantity demanded would be more or less than the percentage decrease in price. Now, here come the tricky questions to gauge your grasp of elasticity. If a product has an elastic demand curve and you decide to reduce price, what will happen?"

A few hands were tentatively raised. "Tell us, Mr. Markham."

"A reduction in price will cause the quantity demanded to increase sufficiently to result in an overall increase in total revenue."

"Good! Okay, now what happens to a product with an inelastic demand curve if the price is reduced?"

Lots of hands shot up. Miss Biles took the initiative. She said, "A reduction in price will still produce an increase in quantity demanded. However, the increase in revenue resulting from selling the greater quantity is not enough to offset the loss in revenue caused by the lower price. Thus, total revenue will decrease."

Moses turned off the projector and continued discussing the complexities of pricing. "Companies change prices over time as variations occur in costs, demand, and the competitive environment."

Moses walked slowly along the front of the classroom as he talked. "Prices also change as products move through their life cycles. There are two strategies for pricing a new innovative product. One is market skimming, which sets a high initial price, then lowers price over time to attract more customers as competitors enter the market. Market skimming makes sense when the consumer's perception of the product's quality and image justifies a high price. Also, the costs of producing small quantities must be reasonable and competitors must be unable to easily enter the market."

"The other strategy for pricing an innovative product is market-penetration, which sets a low price to attract many buyers and gain a large market share. For this strategy to work, production and distribution costs must fall as sales increase, plus the market must be price sensitive."

Moses noticed that several students had started shuffling around in their desks. He checked his watch and, sure enough, it was quitting time. "Well, I see that you are all ready to go. Your homework assignment is on your class syllabus. Adios."

Everyone jumped up and headed out of the classroom. Moses thought to himself that the whole process resembled a cattle stampede in an old western movie.

Chapter 7

Motels are a service that can be seen as three different kinds of consumer products. Some tired motorists are satisfied with the first motel they come to - a convenience product. Others shop for a certain price or facility - a shopping product. Others study tour guides, a seek recommendations, and make reservations - a specialty product.

Jerome McCarthy and William Perreault, Jr.

As Duke was riding his motorcycle to Moses' house, he was thinking how Moses wasn't such a bad guy for an old professor. Of course, Moses wasn't really that old; it was just that all professors seemed old. Then he laughed as he thought that was what he was going to be one day--an old professor--if he could ever get his dissertation written. He knew that many of the students who start dissertations, never finish them. Well, he wasn't going to be in that floundering boat--not after all the hours of course work he had already invested in his quest for the doctorate degree -- the union card to teach at a major university.

Thirty minutes later, Duke was on the professor's doorstep ringing the door bell.

Moses opened the front door. "Greetings, Sir, please enter my humble abode."

"Why, thank you, my good man. Mmmmm, something smells great. Italian?"

"Indeed, follow me to the dining area and let me introduce you to the chef."

Moses continued as they entered the dining area, "This is my daughter, Katie, a promising Italian chef."

"Please, Dad, you're embarrassing me. Don't believe my dad until you taste the lasagna. It's my first try."

"Well, as I was saying, my daughter, Katie, is a worried Italian chef. Katie, this is John Wayne Jones, the computer whiz I was telling you about."

"I'm pleased to meet you, Mr. Jones."

"Duke, please," he interjected. "Dinner smells great."

"I hope you like lasagna." Katie said.

"I love anything that doesn't come wrapped in cellophane," Duke responded with a smile.

Katie told the men to relax in the living room a few minutes while she put the food on the table.

Moses handed Duke a piece of paper. "I just read a thought-provoking story. I think you'll find it interesting."

Duke examined the page on which was printed the following:

What is Success?

In 1923, a very important meeting was held at the Edgewater Beach Hotel in Chicago. Attending this meeting were nine of the richest men in the world: *Charles Schwab*, President of the world's largest independent steel company, *Samuel Insull*, President of the world's largest utility company, *Howard Hopson*, President of the largest gas firm, *Arthur Cutten*, the greatest wheat speculator, *Richard Whitney*, President of the New York Stock Exchange, *Albert Fall*, member of the President's Cabinet, *Leon Frazier*, President of the Bank of International Settlements, *Jessie Livermore*, the greatest speculator in the Stock Market, and *Ivar Kreuger*, head of the company with the world's most widely distributed securities.

Twenty five years later, Charles Schwab had died in bankruptcy, having lived on borrowed money for 5 years before his death. Samuel Insull had died penniless after being a fugitive from justice. Howard Hopson was insane. Arthur Cutten had dies overseas, broke. Richard Whitney had spent time in Sing-Sing. Albert Fall had been pardoned from prison so he could die at home. Leon Frazier, Jessie Livermore, and Ivar Kreuger had each died by suicide.

Each of these men achieved worldly success,

> but each ended his life in tragedy. Making lots of money is fine, but money surely doesn't guarantee a truly successful life. How do you define success?

"That's quite a little essay," Duke commented when he finished reading. "Where did you get it?"

"A colleague gave it to me a few years ago. She saw it in the *Journal of Business Ethics*. I hand out copies to each class I teach. My students usually find it thought-provoking. I want them to know that money isn't everything."

Before Duke could comment further, Katie rang the dinner bell and called, "Dinner is ready."

As they sat down to their salads, Duke tipped his head to emphasize he was listening to the music playing in the background. "Mozart, right?"

"Well, now, aren't you the cultured fellow. I knew you were an unusual character. At least a strange combination of computer jock and motorcyclist. I certainly didn't think you had time for the more refined aspects of Western civilization." Moses smiled as he picked up his salad fork.

"Katie, does your father have a negative image of Ph.D. students? I would have thought that he, being a former student himself, would know that we do not have to fit neatly into one of the two Hollywood stereotypes -- party animal or puny geek."

Moses and Katie both laughed. Duke's stature was certainly not puny. Katie responded, "All I really know is that you were recommended to Dad by an old college buddy. Dad says you know your stuff, and he's disappointed you haven't invited him to try out your motorcycle."

Moses interrupted with a mouthful of salad, "Now that's all true, except maybe the 'disappointed' part. Relieved is more like it!" Duke broke into a big grin.

Moses was enjoying getting to know Duke. Duke was full of vim and vitality, ready to take on the world. Moses was still ready to take on the world; although he had eased off a tad on the vim and vitality stuff. The last few years had been a rough experience, but

Duke's enthusiastic personality was contagious. Funny, at first he didn't particularly like Duke's cavalier attitude, not to mention his intimidating motorcycle. Oh, well, sometimes people are not what they first appear to be.

Katie interrupted his "wool gathering." "OK, guys, it's time to dip into the lasagna. Let me serve your portions. The pan is too hot to pass around the table."

"Thanks," said Duke as he handed Katie his plate. She gave Duke a generous slice, and then took her father's plate and did the same. As they took their first bites, she asked, "Well? Well? Don't keep me in suspense!"

"Delicious," responded Duke while chewing his first bite. "My compliments to the chef."

"Scrumptious, daughter," added Moses.

"I'm so relieved," said Katie. "You can have all you want. I made a ton."

Later, Moses had seconds and Duke had thirds.

As Mozart's fifth violin concerto entered its finale, Duke remarked, "Isn't that great. Can you believe he wrote that and his first four violin concertos before he was 20 years old?"

"Yes, he was a genius," stated Katie. "In fact, he wrote all five violin concertos in less than a year."

"Amazing." said Moses.

"Mozart?" asked Katie.

"No. The way you two have these facts and figures in your heads. All I know is that I like the music."

"Oh, really, Dad. You know all sorts of trivia about Mozart, Beethoven, Bach, and lots of other classical composers."

"Well, it's true that Charlie Brown's friend, Schroeder, and I consider Ludwig Van Beethoven the greatest musician of all time. The fact that he was a German composer, and possibly a friend of my ancestors, has nothing to do with my high regard for his music."

Amused, Duke asked, "So, you know something about your roots, eh? Well, I'm a wee bit of an highlander myself. No great composers I know of, but there was a great poet from Bonnie Scotland by the name of Robert Burns."

"Scotland? Well, well, I knew there was something about you I liked," quipped Moses.

"That's where another branch of our family came from," joined in Katie. "My great-great-great grandfather came to America in the 1830's. Dad has an old family Bible in which one of our ancestors recorded family events, births and marriages and such."

"Well, that's great," said Duke. "I wish I knew more about my family history. Genealogy is fascinating to me. I've heard many stories about my family history, but unfortunately don't have much in writing, like birthdays and marriages. No one seemed to take the time to write down these things in my family. I do know that one ancestor came over in the late 1700's. It seems one of my great-greats supported the attempt of Prince Charlie to claim the throne of England. After which, things didn't go so well for the Scots, and many left for the Land of Opportunity."

"I know about that from English Literature," added Katie. "He was Prince Charles Edward Stuart. Too bad for him and the Scots. The English brutally beat them at the Battle of Culloden Moore. Mid-1700's, I think."

"You have English literature in the ninth grade?" asked Duke.

"Actually it was an advanced literature class back at my junior high in Philadelphia. You learn so much about history from literature, and history is my favorite subject."

"Well, that's only because you haven't had any computer classes yet," Duke said with a laugh.

"Actually, Duke, I've been learning about computers since the first grade," responded Katie.

Moses smiled. "That's right, old man. The modern generation is learning computers in elementary school. Times, they are a-changing."

"Speaking of school, Dad, if you will excuse me, I need to get started on my homework. Can you believe it! School just started and I have a report to write."

"That's fine, honey. I'll get the dishes later." Moses explained to Duke, "Whoever cooks doesn't have to clean up. Katie cooked, so

I'm the kitchen crew."

"Good night, Duke. It was nice to meet you. Don't let Dad talk your ears off."

"Thanks for dinner, Katie, it was delicious."

With that Katie rose from the table and headed to her room.

"You have a great daughter, Moses. You must be a good dad."

"Thanks, I just pray I can be the father she deserves. There have been some tough times since I lost my wife. Hey, would you like some coffee?"

"No thanks. However, being around various Coca-Cola paraphernalia all day has made me want a Coke. Do you have any?"

"Sure thing. Go make yourself comfortable in the living room while I get it."

In a minute, Moses entered the living room holding two tall glasses of ice-clinking Coca-Cola. "It's not a mansion," he said, motioning around the room. "But it meets our needs."

"It looks a lot better than my bachelor pad. Is that your stereo in the armoire?"

"Yes, you want to take a look?"

"Sure," replied Duke as he took his glass. They both walked over to the armoire. The doors were already slightly ajar. Moses opened them completely.

"I purchased all the stereo components: amp, tape player, turntable, and speakers several years ago. Two years ago I acquired the CD player. Would you like to hear something besides Mozart?"

"Do ye have any bag-pipe music for a Scotsman?" Duke tried his best Scottish accent.

"I should get some."

"Well, then, just let the violins play," said Duke.

Moses motioned to the two easy chairs.

"Ahh, this a comfortable chair," remarked Duke as he relaxed on the furniture.

"So where are you from besides Scotland, Duke?"

"I grew up in Wayne County, Mississippi. Believe it or not, the Scottish influence was very strong there. The first school in the county was established in 1812 by the Scots. They didn't even speak English. They spoke Gaelic."

"I know a little about Gaelic," Moses mused. "Eighteen letters in the alphabet, compared to English's twenty-six."

"That's right. One old Scotsman, Sir George MacKenzie said, 'our pronunciation, is like ourselves, fiery, abrupt, sprightly, and bold.' I think Linda must have some Scottish blood."

"Linda?"

"Linda Lou Barfoot."

Moses smiled. "Have you two been spending time together off the job?"

"Yes, I confess. I've been mixing business with pleasure. Linda's a great person."

Moses agreed, "Linda does seem to possess the qualities of a good Scottsman. The Scots were tough, thrifty, hard-working people. They made good pioneers. They were fiercely independent, possessed a strong love of family and country, and had stern moral values."

"Hmmm, haven't changed much have they, Moses?"

"No, I guess not. There's a movement in Scotland even now to separate from Great Britain. Apparently many of them feel they didn't get their fair share of the North Sea oil revenues."

"Are you serious? Could they really separate from Great Britain? The South tried to separate from the U.S. in the American Civil War. The results weren't too good. Citizens of a country ought to work together for the common good."

Moses answered, "I agree. Unfortunately, holding a country together is often difficult. Britain has an especially stormy past since Scotland and England were separate countries for most of their history. They fought many a bloody battle with each other before joining together as the United Kingdom of Great Britain. The British flag is a combination of the old Scottish and English flags."

Moses continued, "One issue of British pound notes features a picture of Robert the Bruce, the Scottish king who thoroughly whipped the English at the Battle of Bannockburn in the 1300's. I saw the battlefield during some free time while attending a conference at the

University of Stirling. It seems that the English executed one of Scotland's major heroes, William Wallace. As a result, the Scots were pretty fired up by the time the English army made it to Bannockburn. There's a great movie about William Wallace, called *Braveheart*. Mel Gibson did an excellent job of directing and acting. Have you seen it?"

"Only about six times," laughed Duke. "It's one of my favorite movies. Besides being tough soldiers, the Scots are renowned as engineers."

"Precisely why the Starship Enterprise's chief engineer was Montgomery Scot," said Moses recalling his favorite TV reruns.

"So you're a Trekker?"

"I like just about any science fiction," replied Moses.

"You know, not too many years ago, computers were science fiction," said Duke.

"The first generation of computers were used in business in the late 1950's." replied Moses, automatically switching to his professor mode. "There are different characteristics of first, second, and third generation computers."

"Let me try to name them, Dr. McDonald. Vacuum tubes, transistors, and integrated circuitry or chip technology. And some say the fourth generation is marked by large scale integration."

"Forgive me, Duke. You're the computer expert. Why am I telling you about computers? You get an A-plus on your quiz."

"Does your consulting work keep you loaded with 'war stories' to share in class?"

"It does. I feel it is unfortunate that most new professors don't have time for consulting or practicing part-time. Too much research pressure. Publish or perish, that's the name of the game today. Like most things in life, there needs to be a balance. Emphasis on research should be balanced by an equal emphasis on teaching."

"I believe that. Remember, I'm in a doctoral program. It's incredible how much I had to read. There's so much in the literature now, so much theoretical stuff with little practical application that I can see."

"Let's face it, Duke, only professors and professors-to-be read much of the academic research. Of course, some of it makes a useful contribution. A doctoral program is somewhat like fraternity initiation, except mental hazing seems to be permitted!"

"I would laugh, but I think you're right, Moses. I will be glad to get the dissertation behind me. Some people told me I shouldn't be taking time out to do anything else, like this consulting job. But, hey, I gotta eat."

"I'm glad you did. I really need your help on this Coke job. What do you think we should tell Ernie Anbert tomorrow? Whatever we decide, I'll discuss it with Chuck Morgan."

"Personally, I don't have a problem with his baseball card program. He seemed to be doing his job. Instead of a coffee break, he simply took a baseball card break. On the other hand, he should not have loaded the program into the Coke system. That should be a strict no-no. He could have kept the program on a disk and used it on his microcomputer. The worst thing he did in my judgment is not informing his superior about the apparent break-in by the person with the unlisted ID. For now, why don't you just tell Ernie that he's officially reprimanded and not to use the computer for unofficial business any more?"

"Sounds reasonable. I'll discuss it with Chuck in the morning. It appears Coke needs more specific written policies on controls and security. As far I can tell, Ernie didn't break any written rules."

"Good documentation of controls is essential to an efficient information system," added Duke. "The programs, control procedures, run manuals, and the like need to be well documented and kept up-to-date."

"What do you think about this apparent hacker? Did he get in through a trap door? And if so, is he a Coke employee or an outsider?"

"Moses, I have a suspicion, and once I check it out, I'll get back to you. There are a number of people who could do it, but why is still the big question. If the hacker limited himself to Ernie's department, all he's looking at are inventory records."

"Could he have sent himself some supplies and then resold them?" asked Moses.

"I don't think so. Coke has a good separation of duties between record keeping and physical custody of assets. Shipping would have to approve that type of transaction, and the hacker wouldn't have the necessary authorization to get that approval. So, I don't think that would work."

Moses and Duke talked for a couple of hours about work, science fiction movies, the Beatles, and which firm makes the best pizza. Duke looked up, "Uh, oh," he said as he noticed the clock on the wall. "I'm afraid I've taken advantage of your hospitality. It's time for me to be moseying on home. Thanks for dinner. A delicious home-cooked meal is a refreshing break from bacheloring."

"I'm glad you could come. I enjoyed our conversation." Moses rose and followed Duke to the door.

"Good night," Duke said as he opened the door.

"Good night, easy-rider," quipped Moses as he watched Duke walk toward the motorcycle parked in his driveway. "An interesting character, that Duke," thought Moses as he closed the door. He picked up the two empty glasses and headed into the kitchen. After cleaning up the dishes, he started for Katie's room to tell her good night, but the phone rang before he left the kitchen.

"Hello," he answered, wondering who would call this late.

"What? How? I can hardly believe it, Chuck. Yes, I'll come by tomorrow." Moses hung up the phone. His little consulting job was becoming rather complicated. The Coke computer system had come down with a pesky virus. "Tomorrow is going to be a tough day," he thought. He went by Katie's room. She was doing her homework while wearing her stereo headphones. He told her good night. Later, in his room, he took a long time falling asleep. He kept thinking that he was overlooking something.

* * *

Chuck Morgan felt mentally and physically exhausted when he heard the soft knock on his office door at 8 am. "Come in," he said. When Moses came in, Chuck motioned to a straight-back chair and said, "Close the door, please."

Moses was always amazed by the impeccable neatness of his friend's office. The desk was always organized. Only a few papers lay on the desktop; apparently they related to the crisis at hand. Next to the main desk was a smaller desk. On it was a Dell microcomputer, a 19 inch monitor, and an Epson printer. Moses noticed the computer was not running. He recalled that Chuck once said, "If there's another way to do it, why use a computer?"

Moses then noticed the photograph on Chuck's desk. It was a family picture of Chuck, his wife, and two daughters. Momentarily, Moses's heart ached as he recalled his late wife. He supposed that he would never really get over missing her. Amazing how fast the memories returned.

"Chuck, you look like death warmed over. Didn't you sleep well?" Moses asked.

"Ha! Sleep? I wish. Computer people from the main office had me up here most of the night. We've been trying to get the system back up. As I told you last night, everything went down. Looks like we may have lost some files."

"Let's start at the beginning, Chuck. What happened to the computer system? What caused it to go down?"

"It was a virus. The night operator indicated that there was a problem about six yesterday evening. By 7:30, things were getting out of control, so he called the systems manager at home. She came up here soon afterwards. She then called in the analysts from our main office about 10 o'clock. I called you soon after that. The virus caused my marketing subsystem"--Chuck waved his right arm--"that is, overseas development, to crash first. Next, the inventory database went down. A couple of other systems were slightly affected before we got things under control."

Moses knew firsthand what a virus could do. Virus programs instruct the host computer to summon stored files. When it does so, the virus program copies itself onto the files. Consequently, the computer's memory degenerates into a big mess. Hackers sometimes create viruses to show off their skills. "How did it get in?" asked

Moses.

"Apparently, someone uploaded it from outside using a modem. You ought to go talk to the systems manager for the details."

Just then Chuck's phone rang. He answered, "Send him in." In a moment Duke opened the door. Before Moses or Chuck could speak, Duke spoke in a rough imitation of John Wayne. "Well, pilgrims, we'd best circle the wagons. We're under attack."

Chuck tried to smile and said, "I'd laugh if I could."

"Duke, I'm afraid our employer hasn't had enough rest. I guess you've gotten the scoop."

"Just that a nasty bug seems to have infected our modern technology. Lucky for Coke they already have on hand two of the world's leading computer consultants."

"Where . . . ." began Moses before realizing Duke was referring to the two of them. "Well, I wish I had so much self-confidence. This job is turning into a little bigger problem than I've had to deal with before."

Moses continued as he looked at Duke, "We need to go talk to the systems manager and find out exactly what happened." He turned back to Chuck and said, "Last night Duke and I discussed our smaller problem of Ernie Anbert. He seems like a fairly decent fellow. We recommend you send him a reprimand letter with a warning not to update his baseball cards inventory or other games on company time. Additionally, you should send a memo to all appropriate personnel not to run unauthorized programs on Coke computers."

"Fine, I will. In the meantime, you computer whizzes can go give my computer a shot of something and get my system back up. More importantly, you can help me revise it so something like this doesn't happen again."

Moses and Duke both left Chuck's office, and went directly to see the systems manager. After talking at length with the systems manager, they went to Moses' work area in the Coke building to discuss the problem.

"So what do you think, Moses? Does the systems manager really have everything under control?"

"He seems competent enough to me. I do appreciate his attitude toward hackers who load viruses into computer systems."

"Lock them up and throw away the key!" Duke laughed. "You remember the big virus incident in November 1988?"

"Oh, sure, the Cornell graduate student who managed to shut down 6,000 computers around the country. The computers were connected through ARPAnet and other E-mail networks in the Internet loop. Some of the nation's top science and research centers were affected. That incident surely made a lot of people start thinking about computer security."

Moses continued, "The worst part is that the guy became a hero to several thousand computer jocks. You know the type I mean. The ones who see security measures as challenges to break. A lot of press coverage focused on admiration of the guy's handiwork, but not his ethics. Some people tried to downplay the seriousness of what he did by explaining that his program was not a virus that destroys data, but a worm that simply uses up storage space. Whatever you want to call it, the bug stopped computer operations at centers all around the country. The creator of a virus can't be sure that it won't get out of control and destroy important data somewhere in a computer network."

"I couldn't agree more." Duke broke into the lecture. "Whether it's a virus program or a worm program, it's a major headache for system users. Admittedly though, a virus that destroys irreplaceable data is much worse than a worm that simply brings the system to a halt."

Moses nodded. "Looks like the Coke system was affected by a virus. But at least there was a backup for most of the data files that were destroyed."

Moses glanced at the Dell personal computer on his desk and said, "Let's see if we can link to the network. The systems manager said it would be up and running by now."

He booted up his computer and logged into the network database. The microcomputer was effectively a "smart" terminal. In other words, it could send and receive information like a dumb terminal connected to a mainframe, but it also could do processing.

The processing ability is what made it a "smart" terminal. One particularly useful feature of using a microcomputer as a smart terminal was the ability to upload and download files between a mainframe and itself.

"What the ...!" Moses gasped after he typed in his user ID, MOSES, and then his password, SCOTLAND. User IDs were assigned by the Coke Systems Department, but users selected their own passwords. The screen displayed the following message:

MOSES McDONALD, QUIT THE JOB OR YOUR
NEXT LECTURE WILL BE YOUR LAST!!

Duke's brow knotted as his eyes focused on the monitor screen. "Someone's gotta lot of nerve," he flatly stated. "Either someone has a warped sense of humor, or this job is becoming rather serious. Looks like we've scared someone."

"Apparently so," said Moses in a slightly shaky voice. His throat was dry and his pulse was racing. He wanted to appear more at ease than he felt. "I don't like being threatened," he said with bravado.

Moses continued speaking. "Professors don't usually have to deal with this sort of problem. I think I'll review all the workpapers, and see if I've overlooked something. I'm sure as heck not going to resign from the job. What really puzzles me is what have we done to upset someone so much? We haven't found anything really bad. I guess we must be close to something, though."

"That's a good idea to take a second look at everything we've done. Moses, do you think we should inform the local authorities about this threat?"

"No, I don't want to do that. I'd probably have to withdraw from the engagement. Remember, I'm just starting up in Atlanta. I need the money. Coke wouldn't want the publicity. Let's just keep this message between the two of us. At least for now. Agreed?"

"Gosh, old buddy, are you sure? This threat seems to have me more worried than you."

Moses was feeling more comfortable again. His pulse had

slowed back to normal. "I'm sure. I doubt whoever made this anonymous threat has any intention to carry it out. Most people who threaten are just bluffing. So, do you agree to keep it confidential?"

"You're the boss. I need the money, too. I just hope we're doing the right thing."

With that Duke walked to the door. Moses followed him.

"I'll see you tomorrow, Duke."

"Okay. I'm going to do some more examination of the password security system. I think I'm close to figuring out who's been doing the unauthorized searches in the inventory system. After that threat, I'm more anxious than ever to know. It could be related."

As Duke walked away, he wondered if silence was the right thing? Should the cops be called? Well, he had given his word. He wouldn't tell anyone without informing Moses first. He stopped fretting and headed toward his work center. When he arrived, he turned on his microcomputer and logged onto the network.

"Well, well," he said to himself. "I'm glad I wasn't left out." The screen bore the message:

JOHN W. JONES, QUIT THE JOB WHILE YOU CAN OR YOUR NEXT COMPUTER LOG-ON WILL BE YOUR LAST!!

A grim expression came over his face. "This situation is getting a little too personal. I won't put up with harassment," he thought angrily. He settled back in his chair and noticed his clenched fists. He laughed slowly. Those fighting instincts were still there. No matter how civilized a person was, just underneath the surface was the deadliest animal on planet Earth. The human brain is what makes man the dominant species, and Duke knew he would have to match wits with the person behind this threat. As adrenalin pumped through his body, he actually felt invigorated by the personal threat. He determined there and then to uncover this anonymous person.

As with Moses's message, Duke knew there was no way to trace it. Both messages were too personal to be random messages. The culprit knew that Moses was a professor, and that Duke was something of a computer guru. Since he couldn't get any fingerprints from the message, he cleared the screen and went to work. Hours passed.

While Duke was busy at his workstation, Moses was working just as steadily. Shortly after lunch, Moses was interrupted by a knock on his office door. "Dr. McDonald, may I speak with you for a moment?"

Moses looked up from his desk. "Yes," he replied.

"Hi, my name is Jacob Goodfellow. I'm with the internal audit department. My supervisor asked me to come by and introduce myself. I've been assigned to assist you in the event that you need the services of the internal audit department. Mr. Morgan told me that you were working on a low-profile investigation.

Moses smiled. "Just call me Moses. I'm pleased to meet you, Jacob. How long have you been with Coke?"

"Just a couple of years, Dr. McDonald." After a momentary pause, Jacob realized his mistake. " A couple of years, Moses." Jacob restated, with an emphasis on Moses' name.

"Well, that's great, Jacob. Where are you from?"

"I grew up mostly in south Texas, near Victoria. I went to college at Texas A&M University in College Station. I majored in accounting and earned a certificate of specialization in internal auditing. There's an informative website about the internal auditing program (http://acct.tamu.edu/smith/eiap.htm). Anyway, after graduation, I was hired to work here in Coke's internal auditing department."

Moses was impressed by the young man's courteous and professional demeanor. He asked, "What exactly do internal auditors do?" Moses was generally familiar with internal auditing but he wanted to hear the young man's perspective.

Jacob thought for a moment before speaking. "Basically, internal auditing is an independent appraisal function established within an organization to examine and evaluate the adequacy and effectiveness of the organization's internal control system and its overall quality of performance. Internal auditing provides top management with analyzes, appraisals, recommendations, and information concerning the activities reviewed. Additionally, internal auditing examines the reliability and integrity of information, compliance with policies and regulations, the safeguarding of assets, the economical and efficient use of resources, and established operational goals and objectives. Internal audits encompass financial activities and operations including systems, production, engineering, marketing, and human resources."

"Internal auditors often specialize in areas such as information systems auditing, compliance auditing, fraud auditing, quality assurance auditing, and environmental auditing. Internal auditors generally report to top management and communicate directly with the audit committee and the board of directors. Due to their expertise and thorough knowledge of operations, internal auditors often fulfill a consulting role to top management."

"That's quite a speech," Moses responded, impressed with the young man's synopsis of his career field.

"I hope I didn't overdo it." Jacob said, a little embarrassed. "I've been studying for the Certified Internal Auditor exam. The CIA exam is internal auditing's counterpart to public accounting's CPA exam."

Moses asked, "Do you have a specialty, Jacob?"

"No, but I'm very interested in fraud auditing," Jacob responded. "One of my friends in the department is a CFE, that is, a Certified Fraud Examiner."

Talking with Jacob was pleasant but Moses realized he had to end the conversation if he was going to get some pressing work completed. "Jacob, thanks for stopping by. I don't need any assistance at this time, but I would appreciate your leaving me your phone number and E-mail address in case I need to get in touch later." Moses handed Jacob a pen and pad of paper.

Jacob wrote down the information Moses requested. Returning the pen and paper, Jacob said goodbye and headed back to the internal auditing department offices.

* * *

After meeting with the internal auditor, Moses worked the rest of the day trying to deduce who sent the death threat. He thought much about the matter as he drove slowly up Martin Luther King's Freeway in the Atlanta rush hour traffic. Based on the work paper review, no one seemed to be seriously threatened by his investigation. Maybe that was the problem. It wasn't in the work papers. As Duke had indicated, perhaps it was tied to the unauthorized searches in the inventory system by the presumed hacker. The hacker was also suspected of the virus incident.

Moses continued thinking of the day's events. After the initial shock, the threat really didn't worry him all that much. He had seen too much of life to be bothered greatly. He had faced other difficult circumstances, particularly the loss of his wife.

He pulled into the driveway, turned off the ignition, and walked to the door. As he unlocked and opened the door, he didn't hear his daughter. "Katie," he called. No answer. "Lord, protect us," he thought as he walked faster than usual to her bedroom. He looked in the doorway.

She looked up, stereo headphones on her head. "Hi, Dad," she said cheerily. "How was your day?" she asked, removing the headphones.

"Fine," he answered, breathing more easily. "Let's get some burgers for dinner. Okay?"

"I would rather have chicken. Are you feeling well?"

"Yes, the traffic was rougher than usual. I'm going to change, then we'll go get burgers and chicken." He turned away from her doorway and walked to his room. He thought, "This job is affecting me more than I thought!"

Chapter 8

There is an immediate need by indigenous management in developing nations to improve their marketing capabilities and knowledge, in order not only to cope with changing consumer needs at the domestic level, but also to catch up with developments and requirements of the markets in developed countries.

Leonidas C. Leonidou,
Middle East Marketing Research Bureau

Moses woke early. He was anxious about his court battle which was scheduled first thing this morning. Even though he had served as an expert witness on other occasions, there were always some butterflies before appearing in court. "Last minute jitters," he thought. "Some people claim a little nervousness helps you do a better job."

Moses had a light breakfast with Katie. She said goodbye and left for school, leaving Moses alone to ponder his court case. He decided to take a cab. He thought, "I want to have a clear head, not one that's been muddled by Atlanta traffic. I can look over my notes on the ride downtown, too." Moses was to be an expert witness for Coke. He called a local cab company, and in a few minutes was riding into downtown.

It was going to be some time before they reached the courthouse in this heavy traffic, so Moses settled back and reviewed the impending case. Five months ago, Coca-Cola was denied a preliminary injunction against Tropicana orange juice. Coke, which produces rival Minute Maid orange juice, was suing Tropicana for a misleading orange juice television commercial. A communication test showed a level of consumer confusion significantly below 15%, and the lower court ruled that this was insufficient for a preliminary injunction. Coke was now appealing to a higher court. In order for the court to grant an injunction, Coke must show that the claim is misleading or false. Coke must also show that they, being the competitor, would suffer irreparable harm (such as loss of market share or goodwill) if the commercial was allowed to continue until after trial.

Moses considered how comparative advertisements were more susceptible to lawsuits since November of 1988 when President Reagan signed the Trademark Law Revision Act. It states that anyone is vulnerable to a civil action who "misrepresents the nature, characteristics, qualities, or geographical origin of his or another person's goods, services, or commercial activities." The revision closed a loophole which existed in the Lanham Act for 43 years. The Lanham Act only prohibited false claims made about the advertiser's goods; it thus failed to consider claims made about a competitor's goods.

The competitor does not have to be explicitly named in the advertisement in order to bring suit. Moses noted that Coke's name was not mentioned in the Tropicana advertisement. The law gives a competitor a cause of action against an advertiser for false statements made about his product in comparison with the goods of a competitor. Thus, general superiority claims such as "most preferred taste" are open to litigation from unnamed competitors. Any competitor who is "likely to be damaged" by a comparative advertisement can bring suit.

Federal law prohibits falsity, but it does not require an advertiser to substantiate his advertising claim. Thus, it is up to the competitor or plaintiff to prove the claim false or misleading rather than the defendant to prove the claim to be true. Based upon Moses' research on court cases, injunctions on advertisements are granted for two reasons. One reason is that the advertisement does not accurately reflect known facts or research data about the product. The other reason is that the advertisement, while literally true, misleads consumers into believing something false about the product. The proof of either of these rests upon the expertise of the plaintiff. Thus, Moses could have a major part in helping Coke win the case. His goal was to help show that Tropicana's advertisement was misleading consumers into believing something false. Judges usually issue comparative ad injunctions after the plaintiff has shown an infidelity in the way the ad communicated the data.

In preparation for the trial, Moses had viewed Tropicana's TV commercial many times on video. The orange juice commercial showed Bruce Jenner, the Olympic athlete, squeezing juice from an orange and pouring it into a Tropicana carton. While pouring, Jenner says, "It's pure pasteurized juice as it comes from the orange." The implication here was that Tropicana was not made from concentrate, unlike other leading brands (i.e., Minute Maid). Thus, Coca-Cola sued.

Moses was so lost in thought that the cab ride seemed to take no time. After paying the cabbie, he walked quickly up the courthouse steps. Following a brief greeting from the attorney outside the courtroom, he was soon on the witness stand.

"Professor McDonald, for the court's record, please state your full name and current address."

"Moses Hubert McDonald, the Third, 1601 Elizabeth Avenue, Atlanta, Georgia."

"Dr. McDonald, we wish to thank you for testifying today as an expert witness about certain advertising claims. First, I have several questions for you concerning your background. Where did you obtain your Ph.D. degree?"

"University of Illinois."

"Where did you receive your MBA degree?"

"Harvard University."

"Where did you receive your bachelor's degree?"

"University of Massachusetts at Amherst."

"Are you listed in Who's Who in America?"

"Yes."

Moses had rehearsed most of these questions and answers before. He liked the grueling task of preparing beforehand and participating in a courtroom battle. There was the challenge to react and respond to the many trick questions asked by the opposing attorney. Probably the stress was not worth the daily fees he received, but he loved it. He sometimes imagined the opposing attorney to be an aggressive college wrestler anxious to pin him to the rubber mat. Moses always pinned his vicious opponent in his daydreams.

"Professor McDonald, what makes you an expert in the area of false or misleading advertising?"

Moses proceeded to list his previous experience and research in the area.

"Dr. McDonald, where are you currently employed?"

"I am a professor at Georgia State University."

The well-dressed attorney turned to the judge and said, "Your honor, I present Dr. McDonald to the court. He is an expert witness in the area of misleading advertisements."

The robed judge turned to the opposing attorney and said, "Mrs. Stroud, do you have any objections to this request?"

The opposing attorney stood up and spoke loudly, "No, your honor."

"So moved. You may proceed, counselor."

"Dr. McDonald, you've done considerable research on how consumers view and react to advertisements. You also have experience in what kind of research and information goes into an advertising claim. As background information, tell us ways in which an advertisement could be false or misleading."

"First, there's the obvious case of contradicting facts," Moses began his testimony. "A claim should be clear and concise and not generalized to encompass more than intended. For example, don't say that a cola has fewer calories than any other drink, when in fact you're only comparing it to other soft drinks. The word 'drink' encompasses many things, including water."

Moses went on, "Research data can be manipulated to misrepresent information. One can pick out only the findings that are favorable or support a certain claim and leave out the negative aspects. Of course, advertisements are not legally required to be 'full-disclosure.' However, the concealment of a fact could potentially create a misleading claim. The makers of an aspirin substitute found this out when the court ruled against them for leaving out some negative research findings which could affect the consumer's health."

The plaintiff's attorney asked, "What about the other end of the spectrum: adding to research findings?"

"Yes, implying more than the research supports is making unqualified claims. Any reported research findings should reflect the limitations which were inherent in the research method. An advertiser cannot take specific research results and embellish them in order to come up with a general superiority claim or any qualified statement. All advertisers want broad, strong claims for their products, but the claims must remain realistic."

"Even an advertisement containing literally true statements can be misleading and thus prohibited under federal law," Moses said. "The federal courts have interpreted the Lanham Act to pertain not only to literal falsehoods but also to implied messages. Through indirect and ambiguous suggestions or innuendo, an advertiser can create an advertisement that misleads consumers."

"Tell the court, Dr. McDonald, how you prove that consumers are being misled by an advertisement."

"Well, you survey consumers to determine what they think an advertisement is saying. In an ad communication test the consumers view an advertisement and report the message it conveys to them. If enough consumers report an incorrect message, the ad is then judged to be misleading."

"How many consumers or what percentage have to be misled by the advertisement to justify the court putting an injunction on it?"

Moses smiled. "That's a million dollar question. There is no totally clear answer. So far, the federal courts are choosing not to set a threshold that automatically qualifies an advertisement as misleading. Each case is decided in context."

"Objection, your honor," the opposing attorney demanded. "The witness is providing law, rather than facts."

"Objection sustained," the judge said. "Dr. McDonald, please keep your testimony dealing with facts. I'll decide what is the law."

"Sorry, your honor," Moses said quietly. "An advertisement can be unintentionally misleading. Advertising content can interact with the beliefs of a consumer in such a manner as to produce various distortions about the advertisement."

The attorney questioned, "Would you explain to the court what is meant by distortion?"

"Distortion occurs while the reader is decoding the advertisement into what he or she perceives the message to be. As a result of the decoding, the message received often differs significantly from the actual message. I've coined the phrase 'distorted decoding' to describe this phenomenon of a consumer improperly reproducing the informational content of an advertisement. Distorted decoding of advertisements affects the consumer's perception and attitude toward the advertisement and related product."

"Let me give you an example from a research study conducted by a doctoral student at Louisiana Tech University. In her dissertation, Smith examined the decoding of literally true advertising claims. The advertisements contained product specific statements. These are true claims about actual product attributes. Half of the consumers in the survey committed a distortion while decoding the advertisements. In other words, the consumer perceived the advertisement as conveying a message which it literally did not present. The consumers attributed the product with additional attributes which the advertisement did not mention. These consumers had a false impression of the advertising content, and thus the product, even though the ads contained only true claims."

"In this study by Smith, the consumers who committed distorted decoding had a more favorable attitude toward the advertisement than those who did not commit distorted decoding. The consumer's attitude became more favorable due to additional qualities he or she mistakenly attributed to the advertisement. Attitudes are important to marketers because of their effect on consumer buying behavior. More favorable attitudes generally lead to more favorable buying behavior. Fishbein's model on attitudes states that an attitude toward a product is a function of beliefs about that product and the evaluation of each belief. In turn, a person's beliefs toward a product are influenced by the content of advertisements."

"Dr. McDonald, you've discussed how the wording of an advertisement can be misinterpreted, what about the visual aspect of an advertisement? Can pictures mislead the consumer?"

Moses nodded, "Yes, pictures can cause a consumer to misinterpret what an advertisement is saying. Pictures can be an outright false representation of the product or they may give a subtle message about the product that is misleading."

"Thank you, Dr. McDonald, you may step down."

Several more people gave their testimonies and presented evidence before the judge finally announced, "The court will recess one hour for lunch." He slammed the gavel. Everyone filed out of the courtroom. Most headed for bathrooms or concessions. Moses followed a small group to the public phones.

After waiting several minutes for a phone to become available, he got one and dialed Duke's number at the Coke building. Moses could not have imagined what was happening at the other end of the phone line.

"What am I doing?" Duke thought. He was leaning very far out the window of his office when the ringing phone startled him. "Man, oh, man, I must be working too hard," he thought as he walked to his desk and picked up the phone.

"Duke, what took you so long?" came the voice over the phone before Duke could even say hello.

"Moses, it's weird. I was daydreaming and looking out my window."

"Right, Duke. So you were daydreaming while I'm downtown busting my buns in a witness box at the courthouse. All the while, I'm counting on my ingenious colleague, John Wayne Jones, to make some serious headway on the job. I called to check-in, and you tell me you're having a weird daydream!" Moses' voice rose a few decibels as he finished his rebuff to Duke.

"No, no, you got it all wrong. I think I'm seriously freaking out." Duke pleaded, although he was a little offended at Moses' lack of compassion. "Your phone call must have brought me back to reality. I was leaning out the window, but I can't remember how I got there. I've been working at my computer all morning. I don't know why I was at the window. No, wait a minute. I remember...I was trying to fly. I thought I was a bird!"

"Weird, very weird, partner. You're sure you're really on the level?" Moses became concerned. He felt bad about his initial gruffness. Moses recalled the warnings that both he and Duke had received on their computers and a sudden idea came to him. "Look, Duke, go over to your computer. Check out the program you're running. I think someone may be sending you subliminal suggestions."

"Now who's weird? Are you serious?"

"Yeah. I'm really serious. I've done some recent reading on the subject. As you may remember, subliminal suggestion is a message flashed on a screen too fast for conscious reading. You know, Vance Packard, *The Hidden Persuaders*. There's never been any positive proof that they have an impact on people. Still the television industry felt compelled to outlaw subliminal suggestions years ago. Maybe our villain saw the 'Mission Impossible' rerun which used subliminal messages to induce a desired response. Just go check out your computer. I gotta go. They're calling everyone back into the courtroom. Duke, be careful."

Moses hung up the phone and joined the crowd milling around outside the courtroom door. He had an uneasy feeling about Duke. He recalled that Vance Packard had given subliminal advertising a bad rap. But millions of dollars of self-help subliminal cassette tapes are sold each year. They provide elevator music combined with inaudible suggestions to lose weight, stop smoking, reduce stress, and so on.

The afternoon session was tedious to Moses after he answered a few simple questions from the opposing attorney. Finally, the judge adjourned for the day, and Moses beat the crowd from the courtroom and was the first to reach the public telephones. He quickly dialed Duke's number. After one ring, Duke picked up the phone.

"Yes." Duke's voice came over the phone line. Moses breathed a sigh of relief.

"That you, Moses?"

"Yeah, I had to make sure you didn't fly out the window. Was the computer involved in your odd behavior?"

"You were right, Sherlock. I used a memory-resident program. That's a program that runs concurrently with another program. I used the memory-resident program to slow processing of the program I was running before my daydream. That's when I saw it. Parts of the subliminal message would appear on the screen for a split second.

When the program ran at normal speed I couldn't see it. But when I slowed down the processing speed, there it was."

"Was what? What was the message?"

"You can fly. Soar like an eagle."

"And you believed that! As big as you are?" Moses laughed now that he was no longer worried.

"The amazing part is how the bum managed to get this message to appear mixed in with the program I was running. This message would appear only a word or two at a time along with pictures."

"Pictures?"

"Yeah. Pictures of birds in flight. I guess I thought I was ready to join them. You know, Moses, this is one unusual job. I'm not sure you're paying me enough. By the way, the same subliminal message was on your computer."

"You're kidding." Moses said in amazement. "We'll talk about your pay later. Besides, maybe we'll write a good novel when we catch the bad guy." He paused. "Duke, I'm glad you're all right. See you later."

"Okay."

They hung up the phones simultaneously.

Moses recalled that most of the subliminal tapes were totally user controlled. He knew that some controversial subliminal communications were being marketed to retailers as honesty reinforcement and theft deterrent systems. Hidden in the pleasant music were such verbal messages as "I am honest" or "I will not steal."

Someone had tried to kill Duke and him with words. What was the old saying? "Sticks and stones will break my bones, but words will never hurt me."

Chapter 9

To err is human. To really foul things up requires a computer.
Anonymous

Moses had precious little break time between the Coke job and his class at Georgia State, not to mention his serving as an expert witness. When he did have a spare minute he tried to catch up on the local news by reading the paper. The feature story in the *Atlanta Constitution* was a perennial one--abortion. Atlanta had received quite a bit of notoriety on the issue. In earlier incidents, the Atlanta cops had apparently been a bit brutal hauling away the "Operation Rescue" pro-life protesters. Very unfavorable news photos of the Atlanta police force in action had appeared in news reports all over the country. News accounts were comparing the Operation Rescue actions to the Civil Rights protests of the 1960's.

Thinking about the protesters brought back memories of Moses' early days. His old friend, Chuck Morgan, had been involved in the Civil Rights movement. Many years had elapsed since those relatively carefree college days. It was interesting how Chuck had brought them back together by hiring him to do the consulting job for Coke. He had first met Chuck at a conference for collegiate business societies at the University of Illinois. By chance, he and Moses were involved together in several workshops and immediately became friends. Moses was an undergraduate at the University of Massachusetts in Amherst at the time. Chuck was attending Northeast Louisiana University in Monroe. They were fraternity brothers; both having joined Delta Sigma Pi (a fraternity for business majors) at their respective universities. Chuck was the first black student to join the fraternity at Northeast. He and Moses had grand dreams about their futures in business and the impact they personally would make. Later, they both were accepted to the M.B.A. program at Harvard. There they became truly close friends while learning to properly pronounce "hah-vuhd" and having numerous Boston adventures together.

Moses went on to pursue a doctorate at the University of Illinois. After earning his Harvard M.B.A., Chuck accepted a job with Kellogg's. Later he switched to his present job with Coke. They stayed in touch through the years, mostly through Christmas cards. Chuck had helped tremendously with Moses' move to Atlanta. The more he thought about the old times, the more he wanted to have a non-business related meeting with Chuck. He rose from the dining table where he was reading the paper and dialed Chuck's home phone number. An answering machine received his call.

After the typical "beep," Moses began his message. "Chuck, old buddy. It's Moses. Guess what? I have to quit! Just kidding. How about having lunch with your only friend? Give me a call." He chuckled to himself as he hung up the phone. He hated talking on those machines, but he thought he had left a good message.

Moses then realized that he was late in leaving for his class.

* * *

Professor Moses McDonald hurried into the old, white block general classroom building. He was already late, so he did not have time to go by his office. Instead he headed toward the room filled with anxious students.

As Moses walked into his classroom he noticed that the overhead projector was already on, and he chuckled when he saw a fallen down stick figure on the screen. It was labeled Dr. McDonald. Scrawled across the top of the screen was: PROFESSORS NEVER DIE. THEY JUST TURN INTO CHALK DUST!

Moses then noticed a group of students at the front of the classroom. As he walked toward the front he asked loudly, "What's up, gang?"

Nancy, a brown-haired student, excitedly explained. "Professor McDonald, Steve just fainted." She pointed to a student laying in a heap on the floor.

Moses rushed over, and felt for the pulse on the student's neck. There was no discernible pulse. Moses next put his right hand on

Steve's forehead. His head was cold. His skin had a bluish-gray cast--probably due to lack of oxygen.

"Has anyone called for an ambulance?" Moses asked sharply. No one spoke. Several shook their heads.

Moses turned to the nearest student and commanded, "Go call an ambulance!"

As the student ran out of the classroom, Nancy pointed to another student, and said, "When Dewayne and Steve went to the front to put on a transparency, there was some white powder on the glass. Dewayne blew the powder off, and it got all over Steve. Steve started coughing and fell down." Moses wished he had taken one of those CPR classes he had heard about. He couldn't ask one of the other students to administer CPR for fear of this unknown white powder affecting them, too.

Moses remembered the computer warning -- Moses McDonald, quit this job or your next lecture will be your last. He always used the overhead projector in his lectures. Someone had tried to kill him. One of his students had gotten caught in the cross-fire.

Duke had received a warning also. What was it? Something about his turning on his computer. Would the culprit put the powder on Duke's computer? I've got to call him!

Moses turned to Nancy. "I have to call someone immediately. Get everyone outside now." And Moses emphasized the word "now." "Do not let anyone get the white powder on them. Nancy, you wait outside the door and tell the paramedics about the white powder." The students began leaving the room. They were visibly shaken.

"Do you think its cocaine?" Nancy asked.

"I doubt it," Moses replied as he rushed out of the classroom. He ran down the hall, up one flight of stairs to his office. He dialed Duke's telephone number at Coke. After about thirty rings, there was still no answer. Where was Duke? He called Duke's apartment. No answer. He tried Duke's office again. No answer.

When he returned to his classroom, all of his students had left except Nancy. And of course, Steve. What a way for his students to get a walk.

The paramedics had arrived. Moses was shocked when the two paramedics pronounced the student to be dead. The coroner was called and an autopsy would be done. Moses shuddered as he considered the full impact of this needless tragedy. He felt nauseated.

After Moses told the paramedics about the white powder, he hurried to his car to drive to One Coke Plaza. He had to warn Duke. "Duke said he would be working late tonight," Moses thought. "Is my warning too late?"

* * *

Duke had heard the ringing of his office phone. It was loud. But he was staring at the white ceiling, while lying on the floor in his office. He could not move his arms and legs. He could not sit up. He could not speak or breathe. But he could think.

When he came into his office ten minutes ago, he immediately saw something that looked like baby powder on his computer. He had first thought that the building custodians had tried cleaning his equipment. But then he recalled the warnings he and Moses had received. Perhaps someone was trying to sabotage his computer.

He remembered taking his handkerchief and carefully wiping off the computer. He didn't consider the powder a personal danger. He shook his handkerchief over the wastebasket. He accidentally inhaled a small amount of dust and immediately noted an odd sensation in his sinuses. After brushing most of the white powder from the keyboard, he flipped on his computer. When he made his first entry, a message flashed on the screen:

DUKE, YOU ARE NOW DEAD!

"Sure I am," Duke thought. However, he felt faint. He didn't have any strength in his arms and legs. He tried to stand up but simply slumped over the keyboard. That was about five minutes ago. The phone was ringing again. "Someone turn it off, please." He wished that he had installed an answering machine.

Linda walked into Duke's office complaining about the phone, just as it stopped ringing. "Duke, are you asleep on the job? Too many late nights for you!" She gently nudged Duke. When he didn't respond, she became alarmed. "Duke, are you okay? What's wrong with you?" cried Linda Lou.

Duke could see Linda Lou, but he could not speak or move. He could not feel Linda Lou's hands shaking him.

Linda walked back to his phone, dialed, and then said, "There has been an accident. Please call an ambulance and have the medics come to Room 423. Duke Jones is sick."

Duke heard Linda Lou leave the room, but she returned shortly with a co-worker. He could hear them whispering--as if he was dead. He wanted to yell but could only think to himself. "I'm not dead. I just can't move. Help me, please."

Soon two medics rushed into the room with a stretcher. The larger medic said, "What happened?"

"I came into Duke's office to answer his phone and found him like this. I don't know what happened."

The second medic bent over Duke and felt his throat.

"There's no pulse." Then the medic tore open Duke's shirt and listened for a heartbeat. "Did anyone here try CPR?" When no one answered, the medic frowned. "Well, it's too late now. He's dead. He must have had a heart attack. You'll need to call the coroner."

"Can't you take the body?" Linda pleaded.

"No, the coroner will have to declare him dead. You'll need an autopsy."

Everyone left. Duke tried to scream. He could not move. Soon he heard someone running down the hall into his office. "Duke. Oh, no. They've killed you, too."

Moses put his hand on Duke's forehead. "It's cold like the student's. Where is the powder?" Moses walked slowly around the office, stopping at the computer. He carefully looked at the system. He noticed that the screen was blank, although the computer was on. There were traces of powder on the keyboard. Moses sat down in a chair and waited. "I should have reported the threat." He dropped his head, feeling much remorse.

Shortly Moses stood up, took out his handkerchief, picked up the phone, and dialed the police. "Hello. This is Moses McDonald, in Room 423 in the Coke Building. I wish to report two murders."

"Yes. Moses McDonald. Room 423. Coke Building. I'll wait for you."

When the police officers arrived, Moses told them about the dead student at Georgia State. He explained about the white powder on the overhead projector and the powder on the computer. He also told them about the previous threats on the computer screens. Be careful, this powder must be deadly. Could you let me know what it is?"

Ignoring Moses' question, the police officer questioned the professor rather bluntly. "You'll remain in town, Dr. McDonald? Right?" Other questions followed.

As they finished speaking, Linda walked into the room, followed by the two paramedics and a man from the coroner's office. "Hello," she croaked to Moses. She looked pale.

Duke was in torment during the ambulance ride. Why couldn't anyone see that he was alive? Maybe he was dead and just didn't know it. He wished now that he had put more thought into his final destination -- heaven or hell.

Duke discovered the cliche' was true. His life actually did flash before his eyes. He suddenly realized that there had been no real meaning to his life. How sad he thought. A person's life should have direction. After all, why are we here? Duke realized that Moses had a handle on what life was about. Duke pledged that if he somehow managed to survive he would have a very serious talk with Moses.

* * *

Shortly after arriving at the morgue, Duke regained control of his body movements. He certainly gave the paramedics a scare! They immediately took him to the hospital where he had to remain for three days.

The poison was tetrodotoxin, one thousand times more toxic than cyanide. The deadly poison was found in the reproductive organs and livers of the puffer fish found off the coasts of Japan. The powder also contained bufotenine and bufotoxin, two ingredients from dried toad skins from Haiti. The toad skin ingredients enhanced the effect of the basic poison. The voodoo powder killed one student and almost killed Duke. He was lucky. He had inhaled only a tiny amount of powder. He had been a zombie for only two hours.

Linda and Moses visited Duke each evening in the hospital. Moses explained in detail the incident that occurred in his classroom. "My student died from the zombie poison. Thank God you didn't."

"I didn't die, but it was an experience I never want to repeat! Do you think Ernie Anbert is involved. Chris Ray Brown? Could it be a business competitor? Who else might be creating this madness?" The trio had no firm answer, but they made a pact to find the killer quickly. Later, Moses found himself in a thought-provoking conversation with Duke concerning some of life's most important questions. Answers to those questions weren't found in college textbooks.

Chapter 10

Why do Japanese cars cost less to make but sell for more? Partly because of the U.S. consumer's costly obsession with product variation and options.

James Cook

Two days later, Moses was busy at his desk when the phone rang. He pressed the speaker-phone button. "Hello, this is Moses McDonald."

"Moses, how would you like to have lunch with an old college buddy today?"

Moses immediately recognized the voice of Chuck Morgan. Feeling worn-out from the happenings of the past few days, Moses was tempted to put off the lunch get-together. However, he also felt a need to talk. "Chuck, that sounds great. What about Ling-Po's Chinese Restaurant?"

"Great. Can you meet me there a little before noon, say 11:45?"

Moses glanced at his desk calendar to be sure he could. "Sure, see you then."

"O.K. Goodbye." There was a click as Chuck hung up. Moses turned off the speaker phone as the dial tone began.

Moses decided to start a new area of the Coke investigation before leaving for lunch. He logged onto the network from his personal computer. He pulled up the sales files. First he looked at the monthly sales summary reports. These were broken down by domestic and foreign sales. He pulled up the foreign reports, which were further categorized by individual countries. He briefly examined each country's sales summary. These reports as well as other financial reports were generated by the firm's accounting information system. The accounting information system coordinated its efforts with the other functional departments such as marketing, human resources, and production, to provide them with the financial information they needed. A business firm depended on teamwork among the various departments. Good communication and a cooperative spirit were required to achieve success.

The sales summary report contained the following information. First, the title of the report and time period covered appeared at the top. This information was followed by columnar headings: location, last month's sales, current month's sales, percent change, year-to-date sales, last year's year-to-date sales, and percent change. The location column listed various city locations throughout the given country. Significant percent changes, monthly or year-to-date, were marked by asterisks on the report. A separate attached report provided explanations or comments regarding the significant changes. For example, one comment was "increase in sales due to onset of tourist season."

After reviewing the most recent month's sales summaries for a number of foreign countries, Moses noticed it was time to leave for lunch. He logged off, picked up his coat, and left his office. The restaurant was a long walk from the Coke building, but he needed the exercise. He had just enough time to walk and make it to Ling-Po's by a quarter till noon. He set a fast pace weaving in and out of the lunch crowd.

As he entered the eating establishment, he caught sight of Chuck sitting at a booth near the door. He glanced at his watch. The time was 11:50. Drat, he thought. He really hated being even a little late.

Chuck saw Moses make his way to the booth. Both smiled as they used the secret fraternity handshake. "Howdy, Moses. You're looking tired. It must be all those tests you have to grade!"

"Speaking of tests, whatever happened to our old chum who got straight A's, Mary Martel?" Moses asked with a grin.

"She and Effie Williams opened a sporting goods store in Denver," Chuck responded.

Moses turned the conversation to the more serious matter of the near-murder of Duke and the tragic murder of the student. During this dialogue, the waiter brought their food.

"Your life is on the line, Moses. If any harm came to you, I'd feel responsible since I recommended you for this job. As I told you when I first heard about these travesties, I'll understand if you want to quit. There are other consulting jobs out there. Most of them are probably a lot less dangerous."

"No, I can't quit. This guy has got to pay. I intend to find out who he is. With Duke's help, plus your Coke colleague, Linda Barfoot, I figure it's just a matter of time before we find him."

Chuck nodded his head. "Him? Could be a woman, equal opportunity, you know. Either way, I'll bet you identify the culprit. You always were a determined fellow, Moses." Chuck smiled.

"Let's change the subject. How's the family? Everything seemed great the night we had dinner at your place." Moses returned the smile.

"I'm happy to say that everything is going fine. Not much has changed since your visit. Barbara Ann is well. She really likes the community and church volunteer work she does. The two girls are all grown up. They were both visiting friends the night you were over. I think I told you that Hannah is in high school and Tracy is attending Emory. She's a marketing major, of all things."

"Did her dear old dad influence the choice of her major?"

"Not really. I suppose she was affected by my work. You know I really do like my job."

Chuck continued. "How do you like Atlanta? Has it been hard as a single parent?" He paused. "That's a dumb question, isn't it?"

"Well, we've managed. Sure, there have been some tough moments. Dan Quayle was right, a child truly needs both a mom and a dad. Katie has adjusted as well as possible. I'm thankful for that. You've been a big help. Your friendship has meant a lot to Katie and me. My consulting business is back in gear. However, this caper at Coke has turned into my roughest job so far."

The two men talked for another half an hour. When they finished, the waiter brought the check and two fortune cookies to the table.

"Well, look at this," Moses stated as he read his fortune.

"It says 'Help, I'm being held prisoner in a Chinese fortune cookie factory.'" He laughed at his own joke.

"Funny," commented Chuck. "Mine says 'Beware of consultants who eat at Chinese restaurants.'" Both men chuckled.

"Chuck, I have really enjoyed this lunch get-together. It really helped me to unload my recent disasters to a sympathetic ear. Katie and I would like to have you and your family over for dinner."

"Dinner sounds great. I'll check with Barbara Ann and get back to you, and you keep me posted on this murder investigation." The waiter walked over to pick up the check and payment. Both men reached for their wallets. "No way. I invited you for lunch, remember?"

Chuck replied, "Well, thanks old buddy. I guess you did."

Moses used his American Express card. "Don't leave home without it." He gave Chuck a comical look. "TV commercials are brain-washing us."

After the waiter returned the card and invoice, Moses filled in the tip and total. As they stood to leave, Chuck asked, "Do you want to walk back together?"

"Sure. I would have walked over with you, but I wasn't sure if I would be at the Coke building this morning. As it turns out, I came from there."

"No harm done. I had to run a few errands downtown before our rendezvous here anyway."

The two men left the restaurant together, returned to the Coke complex, and split up inside the building.

After returning to work, Moses accidentally discovered an old newspaper clipping in one of his desk drawers. The former occupant had apparently clipped an article from a newspaper and left it in the desk. Out of curiosity, Moses picked it up and began reading. The article described Coke's Super Bowl XXIII halftime show. Coca Cola had arranged a 3-D commercial and half-time show.

The company had packaged the 3-D glasses with Coke products. A great deal of publicity had been given to Coke regarding the first live 3-D show and commercial in network history. It was a great marketing idea that incorporated advertising and sales promotion while creating publicity due to its ingenuity. Moses knew that advertising is defined as any paid form of nonpersonal presentation and promotion of ideas, goods, and services by an identified sponsor. The half-time show was a successful sales promotion. The publicity generated was a form of public relations which builds good relations with a company's public.

Coke used television as the media for its commercials. Moses mentally reviewed the factors affecting media choice: the nature of the product, costs, characteristics of the message, and the media habits of the audience one wants to reach. Several factors were considered in choosing the Super Bowl as the media vehicle. The cost per thousand people reached and the costs of producing the commercials were expensive. Noncost factors were also important: credibility, status, and reproduction quality. Cost figures must be adjusted for audience quality and attention. The commercials were copy tested beforehand to determine whether the ad was communicating well.

Using the Super Bowl gave Coke all the benefits of advertising: repeated communications, expressiveness, and a large audience. The commercials used persuasive advertising which is effective for products with heavy competition. The "cola wars" -- the comparison of cola brands -- is a battle in persuasive advertising. Diet Coke's jingle, "Just for the taste of it," had been sung by a variety of celebrities including the Pointer Sisters, Jessica Rabbit (from the Disney movie "Who Framed Roger Rabbit"), and Whitney Houston.

In 1989 alone, Coca-Cola used 27 celebrities to help sway consumers. These included Chris Evert, Phylicia Rashad, Jerry Hall, Vanna White, and Sugar Ray Leonard. However, the next year Coke discouraged using simple endorsement spots. Instead, the company favored more creative commercials. An example would be the ads that featured Art Carney as a lovable grandfather. Traditionally, the two rivals, Coke and Pepsi, react to changes in each other's advertising.

Moses recalled the January 1989 Super Bowl. It had been one of the best Super Bowls ever. San Francisco beat Cincinnati with a last minute touchdown pass by Joe Montana. Paul Harvey had even described the winning play in his daily radio show, "The Rest of the Story." It turned out that the players had gotten mixed up. The winning score had resulted from the players running the play wrong. Moses thought how funny it was that goof-ups occasionally work out for the best.

Moses returned to his examination of the Sales Summary

Reports. He noticed that Coke had operations in a number of former communist countries in Eastern Europe. He recalled that Duke and Linda would soon be traveling to Poland together. Coke wanted to establish a plant there. Linda would be involved in the negotiations. Moses still wasn't sure exactly why Coke wanted Duke to go along. Since Duke's near-death incident, Linda had been very attentive to Duke. They went out together almost every evening. Moses thought there was nothing wrong with that; he sometimes wished there was more romance in his own life. However, he felt he needed more time to adjust to his wife's death.

As Moses looked at the reports on his PC, he continued his earlier procedure to scan the "percent change" columns for the monthly sales changes and year-to-date sales changes. He noted the significant percent changes, marked by asterisks. A separate attached report provided comments and explanations for the significant items. On one of these "comment" reports he saw a comment for the year-to-date change that he had not seen before--"same as last month." Since he had not read a "same as last month" explanation before, the oddity of it made him curious. Consequently, he pulled up the preceding month's report to see what had occurred at that time to cause a significant change in the year-to-date sales.

"Now this is getting interesting," said Moses to himself as he looked at the prior month's sales report. On that report, as for the current month's report, there was no significant change from the prior month's sales, but the year-to-date sales were down by 70 percent from the prior year's year-to-date. And again, there was that explanation--"same as last month." He pulled up the preceding month and again found the same explanation. He wondered, "How far back am I going to have to go to get an explanation other than 'same as last month?'" He pulled up the next prior month's report; that is, three months back from the current month's report, and found the following comment: "New machines. Not working properly."

Moses realized his knowledge of Coca-Cola's dispensing machinery was rather limited, but that explanation just made him all the more curious. He began wondering how that could explain the unusual change. "How could new machines cause a drop-off in the month's sales four months in a row? If there was a problem, it should have been fixed before now. However, it was in a formerly communist country. Perhaps, some local government official was actually causing the problem. Or perhaps, the local help was slow to fix an American firm's equipment." He made a mental note to investigate further.

Moses looked at his Mickey Mouse watch and realized it was time to leave for his class at Georgia State.

* * *

As Moses entered the classroom, he knew it would be difficult to have a normal lecture so soon after Steve Jackson's tragic death. What really grieved Moses was the fact that Steve had died as a result of the misfortune of being in Dr. Moses McDonald's class. None of the other professors had provoked any homicidal maniacs.

Moses could not bring back the dead student, but he would not rest until he found the student's killer. He noticed on his class roster that Dewayne had dropped the class. Poor Dewayne would always feel guilty that he had been the one to blow the voodoo power off the overhead projector and onto Steve. Moses decided that he would try to have a visit with Dewayne. After all, if anyone was to blame, Moses thought it wasn't Dewayne but Moses himself.

"To start, let's cover a few basics regarding financial statements. Financial statements for businesses include: 1) balance sheet, 2) income statement, 3) statement of cash flows, and 4) statement of retained earnings."

"First, the balance sheet shows the total assets, total liabilities (debts), and total equity (net worth) of a business. The balance sheet shows the financial position of the business at a specific point in time."

"Second, the income statement shows the net income of the business. Net income is revenues minus expenses. The value of a company as an investment depends largely on its future profits (net income)."

"Third, the statement of cash flows depicts the cash inflows and outflows. The chief difference between the income statement and the cash flow statement is that revenue and expense items are included on the income statement as they are accrued (incurred), which is not necessarily when cash is received or disbursed. Many small businesses fail not because of lack of profits but because of poor cash flow."

"Fourth and finally, the statement of retained earnings shows the change in retained earnings from the beginning of a period to the end. Basically, a firm can either retain its earnings (net income) to expand its operations or pay out its earnings as dividends to shareholders."

"Financial ratios assist investors in determining the financial strength of a potential investment. Analysts use many financial ratios. One of the most prominent financial ratios is the price to earnings or P/E ratio which is widely used by analysts in assessing the investment potential of different stocks. It is calculated by dividing the market price of the stock by the earnings per share."

$$\text{Price to earnings ratio} = \frac{\text{Market price of stock}}{\text{Earnings per share}}$$

"One of the difficulties investors face in today's global marketplace is that financial statements of firms based in different countries are not necessarily prepared according to the same accounting rules. The International Accounting Standards Committee and the International Federation of Accountants are endeavoring to develop harmonized financial accounting and auditing standards, respectively, to meet the worldwide demands."

"Worldwide acceptance of international accounting standards will ultimately be determined by the International Organization of Securities Commissions and the individual securities commissions, which make up the IOSCO. Over 60 securities regulatory agencies worldwide comprise the IOSCO, including the U.S.'s Securities Exchange Commission. A major objective of the IOSCO is the facilitation of cross-border securities offerings and multiple listings without compromising the financial statement information provided."

Moses looked out at his 26 students, "I'd recommend taking notes." A person on the back row caught Moses' attention. The person was wearing dark sunglasses. Moses didn't recall ever before seeing the gentleman in the sunglasses.

Moses glanced out the window and saw people rushing by on the sidewalk. The class had started at 5:30pm in the general classroom building on the Georgia State University campus. He thought, "The word 'campus' may not be the best description of Georgia State. Combat zone, maybe." Being on the quarter system, this class met twice a week, two-hours and fifteen minutes per class. Moses was a subway stop professor. He continued, "Why does a company want to seek new marketing opportunities here or abroad?"

As he walked over to place his first overhead slide onto the projector, he noticed that it was bolted to the table. He sighed softly.

"Because stagnation is equivalent to death in the area of marketing. Companies may choose their marketing strategy from among several alternatives. One strategy is market penetration, which seeks to increase sales of existing products in existing markets through more aggressive marketing efforts. Or a growth strategy may zero in on identifying new markets for existing products; this is called market development. The reverse of that is product development, where new or modified products are sold to existing markets. The final growth strategy is diversification, where new products are offered to new markets, either by developing businesses in industries outside of the firm's normal operations or by buying existing businesses."

A student raised his hand, and Moses responded. "Yes, Mr. Pride, do you have a question?"

"How does a company know which strategy to use or which products to offer?"

"Good question," said Moses. "Marketing research is the answer. The first step to take is defining the problem and determining the objectives of the company. For example, what are the characteristics of your current market, what does the customer think of your current products, is there an unfulfilled need, where is the growth potential, and so forth."

"The second step is developing the research plan; objectives must be translated into specific information needs. Will you need secondary data -- uh, information that has already been gathered for some other purpose -- or primary data, which is information you collect first-hand. There's different approaches to primary data collection." Moses wrote the three items on the board: observation, survey, and experimental.

Then he continued. "The third step is implementing the research plan. The final step is interpreting the findings."

Moses noticed that the gentleman was still wearing sunglasses and was not taking notes. "People can be unpredictable. That's why marketing research is so important in discovering needs, reactions, preferences, and so on. Cultural factors exert the broadest and deepest influence on consumer behavior. Look at how many new or revitalized products came about in America due to increased concern over health."

"In trying to predict what people will buy, it is beneficial to look at the actual buying decision process. The buyer's decision process starts with problem recognition which precedes the purchase." Moses cleared his throat. "The buyer perceives a need. Marketers try to increase demand by determining what factors evoke this problem recognition."

"The buyer may then search for information on available products and features. This is called information search. However, the buyer may not need additional information to undergo the next step in the buying process, which is the evaluation of alternatives. The buyer then makes the actual purchase decision. Post purchase behavior is also of interest to the marketer who wants repeat customers. A marketer will strive for post purchase satisfaction rather than cognitive dissonance." Moses wrote "cognitive dissonance" on the board. "That's where the buyer is unhappy with his decision, or wonders whether he made the right choice."

After pausing for a moment so the students could copy the marketing buzz words, he continued. "Humans are highly complicated beings; thus, there is an entirely different decision process for new products. Of course we have to give it a different name -- the adoption process. Here, the consumer must first become aware of the product. Then his or her interest must be piqued. The consumer evaluates the product and may or may not buy the product on a trial basis. If the consumer decides to be a regular user, he has adopted the product."

"Let me give you an example. In 1985, Coca-Cola's marketing

research on a new product, called 'New Coke,' was obviously faulty in predicting its adoption response. Consumers were so upset about the original-formula Coke being replaced, that the old Coke was brought back after just three months. New Coke remained on the market, but it never lived up to expectations. Four years later it had only 1.5% of the cola market. Now, it's a thing of the past." Moses smiled and said, "New Coke was given the title of Edsel for the 1980's."

"New Coke did have a positive affect on the company's market share overall. The tremendous amount of publicity generated about the withdrawal and subsequent return of old Coke boosted consumers' awareness of the company. Resulting from the halo effect, the market share for all of Coke's brands increased."

Moses turned a page in his lecture notes. The gentlemen in the sunglasses was starting to unnerve Moses. He seemed to follow Moses' every move but still wasn't taking notes. The only time the man's arm moved, was to check his watch periodically. Moses began to imagine some worst-case scenarios. He mentally noted all the possible exits from the classroom. The image of his dead student kept coming to mind. However, he still had a class to teach and students awaiting further instruction. He resumed his lecture.

"Retailing combines all the activities involved in selling goods or services directly to final consumers for their personal, nonbusiness use. Retail stores can be classified in several ways: (1) by their prices, (2) by the amount of service they offer, (3) by the length and breadth of their product lines, or (4) by the control relationship among their outlets. Let's look in more detail at the last classification." Moses slipped on another overhead showing these classifications in neat detail:

Types of control relationships among retail outlets:

1. Franchise -- an independent (franchisee) buys the right to own and operate one or more units in a franchise system. The franchisee and franchiser have a contractual association.

2. Corporate Chain -- contains two or more outlets that are

commonly-owned and controlled; has central buying and merchandising; and sells similar lines of merchandise. Chains can take advantage of economies of scale in buying and in promotional expenditures.

3. Voluntary Chain -- a wholesaler-sponsored group of independent retailers that performs group buying and common merchandising. A retailers cooperative is a group of independent retailers that set up a jointly owned central wholesale operation and conduct joint merchandising and promotion efforts.

After reviewing each relationship, Moses opened the floor to questions.

"Dr. McDonald, I've read that Eastern Europe may be shaping up as a new frontier for franchises. What is your opinion on this?" A student asked from the back of the room.

"A very good question. Let's first look more closely at the advantages of a franchise. The franchisee is allowed the use of a trademark, trade name, patent, marketing guidelines, a process and/or a recipe. Thus, franchisees are immediately given know-how and marketing knowledge that otherwise would take years to develop. In a very positive way, this transfer would suit the needs of entrepreneurs in a newly developed free-market economy."

Moses paused, then resumed. "Franchises in the United States account for one-third of all of the consumer purchases. What are some well-known franchises?"

Several students spoke out, "McDonald's, Jiffy-Lube, Burger King, Dairy Queen, Domino's Pizza, and Subway."

"There is a wide variation of costs for franchises. A few years ago, a Subway franchise could be bought for about $7,500 plus an 8% royalty and a 2.5% advertising royalty. This is one of the less expensive franchises," said Moses. "A McDonald's franchise cost over $125,000."

Moses continued as he paced the floor. "Business format franchising has proliferated in the U.S. Here, a franchiser provides a marketing strategy and plan, an operating manual, and a uniform business concept. There does not have to be a sale of the franchisor's product. Examples of this are convenience stores, auto productions and service stores, real estate agencies, accounting firms, beauty salons, and hotels."

"Now, let's look at the opportunities for franchises in Eastern Europe. Currently, joint ventures are more common over there. However, these ventures could open the door to franchises. McDonald's and Baskin-Robbins have both entered Russia through joint ventures but are making long-term plans to franchise. Baskin-Robbins' joint venture began business in 1992 with a thirty million dollar plant. They will be introducing a new flavor called Gorba Chocolate!"

"Since franchises include set-up and marketing know-how, they may play a major part in creating a new class of Eastern European entrepreneurs. A big problem will be finding people who can afford to buy a franchise. Another problem for the franchisors is that they may have to spend millions of dollars to set up reliable and quality sources of supply which Eastern Europe is lacking. For example, McDonald's had to build a bakery and a meat plant to ensure quality supplies for their restaurants. This problem, of course, can add a year or more to the start-up time for a franchise. It could take twice as long to start a franchise in Eastern Europe as opposed to the U.S.,where most supplies are already available."

"The success of the McDonald's restaurant in Moscow has drawn the attention of many franchisers. The 700-seat restaurant has been packed ever since it opened in January, 1990. The people are willing to wait in line for hours just to get in. The waiting line is said to be 500 yards at times. McDonald's partner in this joint venture is the Moscow city authorities. McDonald's is building 20 more restaurants in Moscow."

A student added to the discussion, "A company right here in Atlanta, Zenox Inc., is planning to franchise in Russia and Hungary with the Payless Rent-a-Car System and Mister Donut outlets. They have paid $180,000 plus royalties for the rights to these franchises. In turn, Zenox plans on setting up joint ventures with foreign partners to sell the franchises to Eastern Europeans."

Moses loosened his tie. "You have to be willing to make a long-term investment if you want to reap any profits from Eastern Europe. It's not the place to make a quick buck. Many of the structural needs of a business are not available, such as a good telephone or fax network. Hard currencies are in short supply there, and repatriating profits back to the U.S. may be a problem due to nonconvertible currencies and currency controls by the government. As with any new venture, some people will turn a good profit and some people will lose their shirts."

Moses checked his watch, "We'd better get back to our discussion about retailing in general. Any other questions regarding the classifications listed on the overhead transparency?"

A male student on the third row asked, "Where do vending machines fit in?"

"They are a form of non-store retailing," Moses responded. "Other classifications of non-store retailing are door-to-door sales and direct marketing. Direct marketing uses various media: direct mail (which includes catalogs), telemarketing (telephone), and television (which includes home shopping channels and order-by-phone commercials). There is also electronic shopping via the Web which links consumers to sellers' computerized information and order-taking systems."

Moses was interrupted by a secretary from the Business Department at his classroom door; she motioned for him. "I'm sorry to interrupt Dr. McDonald, but you have a phone call from a man named Duke. He said it's an emergency and insists on talking with you." Moses felt his pulse quicken. After asking his students to excuse him for a moment, Moses ran down the corridor to the phone.

"Duke, what's wrong?" Moses asked breathlessly.

"I've got something." Duke said quietly into the receiver.

"Could you be a little more informative," Moses demanded irritably. "You just pulled me out of the middle of class!"

"I didn't want to risk missing you," Duke retorted. "This is really big. I can't say any more over the phone, I'm at the Coke building. I'll come over to your house after your class. I think I know whodunit. See you soon."

Moses hung up the phone, perplexed. He suddenly remembered the strange gentleman in the sunglasses. Moses felt an increasing concern about leaving his students and hurried back to class.

Upon entering the classroom, Moses immediately looked to the back row. The man in the sunglasses was gone. Moses surveyed the rest of the room; everything seemed normal. His concern mounted but there was nothing to do but continue teaching.

Moses began, "Once out in the market, the typical new product has a life cycle made up of four stages." Moses counted on his fingers. "First is the introduction stage where profits are low due to large start-up costs. There is little competition at this time. Second is the growth stage. Sales and profit are growing; thus, competitors are increasingly drawn to the field. The maturity stage is third. Competition is strong and sales growth has slowed down. Marketers try to increase sales by improving the product, by changing price, promotion, service, or distribution. The final and fourth stage is the decline where, you guessed it, sales are declining."

Moses paused and pulled out his distribution channel notes. "You can gain or lose competitive and cost advantages depending on your product's distribution channel. A distribution channel is the set of people that take title, or assist in transferring title of a product as it goes from the producer to the consumer. Middlemen receive a lot of flak, but they are simply carrying out the following tasks which must be done by someone: physical distribution, financing, risk taking, contact, matching, negotiation, research, and promotion."

Moses discussed a couple of distribution problems before it was time to dismiss class. He was very anxious to get home.

Chapter 11

Sales forecasting is difficult with new products. Cajun Cola, a spicy Louisiana-based soft drink, sold more during the first week of test marketing than the company had expected to sell the entire first month.
Becky Shockley

"Don't you get it, Moses? This guy has to be our man. He's been retired for a few years, and he's beginning to feel pinched living on his fixed retirement income. Then, presto-whammo, he gets an idea--steal some valuable information from my old employer and sell it to a rival company."

"Whoa, buddy. I understand Kirby Forrest was in charge of programming when Coke installed their last system, but please explain again why you think he's the hacker."

"Okay. First of all, he's the only one with sufficient knowledge of the system to be able to do it. We know the hacker used a Trojan-Horse type of trap door to get into the system. Only a programmer with intimate knowledge of the system could do that. But to move around in the system would require more than just the getting-in kind of knowledge. It requires knowledge of additional passwords, and more importantly, how the system is configured. This guy would know that. But here's the clincher--he's using the same account number he had twenty years ago. I went back through the old master lists of valid user-IDs and related passwords since Coke got their first dial-in computer system. His old ID and password were there and match the ones the hacker used."

"Duke, gimme a break. He couldn't be that stupid. Why would he use a number that's bound to give him away?"

"I thought about that. Two reasons. One, it's twenty-years old. Who'd think to look through the old records except a genius like myself. Two, he's desperate and couldn't break into the system any other way. Also, we still can't prove he stole anything of value yet. All he has done is retrieve tons of inventory records data, primarily about shipments received. But here's where it gets interesting. I have a theory. Don't laugh."

Moses smiled a crooked smile. "Laugh. I can't laugh. I'm waiting for you to make sense of all this for me."

"The Diet Coke formula. He's after the Diet Coke formula!"

The two men stared at each other for a few moments.

Moses groaned. "Oh, man! You're kidding me. Water, sugar, carbon dioxide, and the Seven X." He started laughing.

Duke just stared at Moses. "Would you stop that. Don't you see, he's after the Seven X part of the formula. Listen to me."

Moses got the hiccups. He couldn't stop laughing, although he was laughing less hard now. He knew that carbon dioxide gave coke its fizz, and the color of coke came from caramel. How the rest of the ingredients fit together to make a tasty soft drink was one huge mystery.

Duke continued, "The inventory records are the key. Kirby Forrest worked for Coke for almost forty years. Don't you think he was aware of opportunities for industrial spying. The diet soft drink business is super-competitive. It's a war out there. Diet soft drink users are the fastest growing market segment. They account for about 30% of the soft drink industry's sales. Diet Coke is the leading diet soft drink. Diet Coke and its caffeine-free partner hold more than an 11% share of the $43 billion soft-drink industry."

Duke paused, looked around, and spoke softer. "I've been reading up on this bombshell of Coca-Cola's. Ironically, the Diet Coke formula originated in a laboratory that was trying to perfect the taste of another once-popular Coke product: Tab. For a year and a half, Diet Coke was a top secret project here at Atlanta headquarters. Papers were collected and shredded after every meeting. The project went by a code name that was periodically changed. The initial code name was Harvard because Sergio Zyman, the Coca-Cola project leader at the time, gave up a job at Harvard University to work on Diet Coke."

"After the formula was perfected, a marketing strategy was designed to introduce Diet Coke. Of course, the target market for Diet Coke was the diet soft drink users. Coca-Cola positioned the new product on its good taste and planned on competing with Pepsi's sweeter taste. A key goal of Diet Coke was to capture a large share of the market."

Duke started circling the room. "Coca-Cola pledged to spend at least $30 million in advertising for Diet Coke's introductory year. The company has maintained high spending levels for advertising."

"When Diet Coke was ready for the world, boy, did it have a great send-off! It was the industry's most elaborate introduction for any product." Duke began waving his arms around for emphasis. "On July 29, 1982, Coca-Cola hosted a Radio City Music Hall gala for some 6,000 people. A towering 14-foot-high replica of the Diet Coke can was raised from the orchestra pit. Entertainment was supplied by a 40-piece orchestra and the Rockettes. The event was filmed and inserted in Diet Coke's introductory commercials. Afterward, the whole audience was bused to a pier on the Hudson River for a food festival costing around $100,000."

Duke was practically ranting and raving by now. "The Diet Coke formula is like a gold mine. Diet Coke is the nation's third largest-selling soft drink, behind only Coca-Cola Classic and Pepsi. The company thinks that within the next decade, Diet Coke will surpass Pepsi as the No. 2 soft drink in the U.S."

Duke stopped talking and looked squarely into Moses's eyes. "Someone's trying to steal the Diet Coke formula and we got in the way."

Moses frowned. "You're serious, aren't you?" he asked.

"Dead serious. We're in the middle of some dangerous corporate espionage. Whoever's behind it has tried to kill me twice. I'm still afraid to use baby powder."

Moses was taken aback by that statement. "All right. Let's assume you're correct, just for the sake of discussion. How does Kirby Forrest get the Diet Coke formula from the inventory records? The formula is one of the world's most highly guarded corporate secrets. I reckon the Colonel's secret recipe of 11 herbs and spices is the only thing even close in terms of corporate secrets."

"Thanks for hearing me out," Duke responded with a bit of indignation. He was a bit miffed from Moses' unnecessary laughter.

"I didn't understand the significance of the inventory records at first myself, but as I pondered over it day and night, it finally occurred to me. Forrest is analyzing the records to derive the Coke formula."

"How?" Moses asked.

"By accumulating all the inventory records since 1982, when Diet Coke was introduced, and by being intimately aware of Coke's production cycles, Forrest can determine exactly what combination of ingredients is necessary to make the world's most popular diet soft drink. He can then sell the formula to the highest bidder in the industry."

"Pepsi?" Moses responded.

"Perhaps. Or some newcomer to the diet soft drink field. Once in a while a new brand pops up. Most only last a few years. Rarely do any make a profit. People know the Coke name, and they just keep coming back to it after trying the no-names for a while."

Another possibility occurred to Duke. "Perhaps someone in a foreign country is interested in buying the Coke formula. China? India? Russia? Remember India once kicked Coke out. India has its own brand of cola, called Thumps-Up, I believe. Perhaps, there are some people who don't want the Coca-Cola Company operating in India or making any profit there."

"Well, you have me interested, Duke. A foreign entanglement. It's quite a theory, barely plausible. If all you say is true, why did Forrest unleash the virus into the system?"

"Elementary, my dear professor." Duke looked like a bloodhound on the scent. "Forrest found out about our investigation, and he decided to cover his tracks. Did you know that the Coke system staff could not find back-ups for some of the destroyed files? Fortunately, yours truly had downloaded some of the crucial ones back at the beginning of our investigation, such as the old master lists of user-IDs and passwords I just mentioned."

"But what made him so desperate that he tried to kill us?" Moses interrupted.

"I suppose he thought we were going to stop his money-making plans from coming to fruition. Maybe he thought our search was aimed specifically at him? Maybe he just didn't like our looks? Maybe we don't know the whole story yet, but I have a plan to get some hard evidence to prove he's the hacker."

"Well, go on, don't leave me hanging."

Duke eagerly continued. "First, we arrange to have the phone lines monitored. Next time he logs on, we will have the call traced to his house. That's the main strategy. But being the resourceful private eye that I am, I also have a back-up plan. I have the guy's address, and I'm gonna tap into his computer system."

"Tap in? You think he has a dial-in service on his PC?"

"I doubt it. But that's not how I'm getting into his castle." Duke lowered his voice to a whisper. "I purchased some electronic eavesdropping equipment, my friend. The stuff cost me $500. You'll see it on my next expense report. The equipment consists of a battery-powered TV set, a TV antenna, and some basic electronic gear. Primarily a couple of oscillators."

"You're beginning to sound like James Bond. How does this spy stuff work?"

"Well, first I locate where Forrest is living. Then, I park in front of his house and tune into his PC's display screen. Most computer systems emanate electromagnetic radiation from the circuitry and from their CRTs. The CRT--uh, that is, cathode-ray tube--is what shoots the beam of electrons that form the image on the monitor screen. My spy gear will allow me to tune into that signal. If all goes as planned, I'll be able to see exactly what Forrest sees on his screen. Also, I plan to record it on a portable VCR to further prove his guilt."

Duke paused in his monologue for Moses' reaction. Moses was still trying to digest this new information, so Duke continued. "By the way, I'll need to rent a van to work from. My bike isn't big enough to hold all this gear, let alone to do my surveillance secretly, if you know what I mean?"

Moses began slowly smiling and shaking his head. "This investigation is really getting crazy." He began humming the theme from the classic TV series, "The Twilight Zone." Duke joined in. They both laughed.

After discussing some practical details of the spy caper, the two men said goodbye. Moses meant to discuss the unusual sales summary report from the Polish location, but he forgot to bring it up during all of Duke's revelations regarding the former coke executive. Well, he'd try to remember to discuss it before Duke went overseas with Linda.

* * *

On the drive home, Moses' thoughts turned to his daughter. She was spending the night with a new-found friend from school. Katie had made this arrangement after Moses had been asked to help teach an international business seminar in Washington, D.C. He was taking an afternoon flight from Hartsfield International Airport to National Airport in Washington, D.C. The seminar started the next day at 8 a.m. He knew Katie was old enough to take care of herself when he was out of town, but he preferred her to stay with someone when he had to travel overnight. He had given Katie his phone number for the Hyatt Regency in Crystal City. Crystal City is a conglomeration of hotels and shops very close to National Airport.

Traffic was heavy; at noon the lunch crowd was out in full force cruising the streets in their automobiles. Moses had observed that normally sane drivers often turn into maniacs when they are on a quest for food. One such road warrior was advancing on him quickly from the rear. In his side mirror, Moses saw a dark blue sedan swerving in and out among the slower cars on the four-lane road. Moses prudently decided to move into the right lane and allow the speeding car easy passage. Completing the maneuver, Moses relaxed a little. Without warning, Moses was jarred by a hard impact on the drivers' side of his car. The next thing he knew was that his car was barreling down the shoulder of the busy thoroughfare, not a good situation. Most distressing, however, was the abandoned pickup truck parked on the shoulder less than 50 yards in front of him. He slammed on his brakes and skidded to a stop less than a foot from the pickup. He tried to calm his shaking body. That speeding maniac, who was now completely gone from sight, had side-swiped him!

Moses cautiously moved all of his body parts to check for injury. Thanks to his seat-belt, he apparently sustained only a jolt to his nerves. Opening the car door, he inspected the vehicle. His car was in need of a little paint and dent repair, but the damage wouldn't hamper the car's driving ability.

Moses continued the drive home at a slower pace with his eyes constantly surveying the surrounding traffic. He didn't want to be paranoid, but he suspected foul play. The reckless driver had plenty of room to avoid the "accident," and he didn't stop after hitting Moses. On the other hand, hit-and-run drivers aren't uncommon. After events of the past week, everything seemed rather ominous. Well, he'd get Duke's opinion about the traffic mishap.

When Moses reached his house, he related the incident to Duke over the phone. Moses was surprised by Duke's reaction. Duke quickly dismissed any thought of Moses' safety and spent the rest of the time questioning whether Linda's life was in danger. Duke wondered if he should be doing more to protect Linda from possible harm. Moses didn't stay on the phone too long; he had to pack for his trip.

Duke was in a terrible emotional state. He knew what the problem was. He had fallen in love with Linda Lou. He knew it was love, not infatuation. He wanted to give, not get. Duke was moonstruck. He was shot through the heart by Cupid's arrow.

Duke had dated several women over the years, but had never experienced the totally vulnerable world of love. Duke spoke out loud. "I'm not a teenager. Why can't I handle this? Because love is a dangerous, emotional feeling. Dangerous?" He was now actually hearing the words in the songs on the radio. That was a new experience for Duke. When he heard certain songs, he would think of Linda Lou and get goosebumps. He thought that goosebumps at his age were ridiculous.

If he was driving down Martin Luther King Freeway and heard certain songs, his chest would swell-up. He would begin waving his hand and arm in rhythm with the music. Yes, dangerous if someone thought he was motioning to them.

Duke was waking earlier in the morning. He would wake-up in the middle of the night. He needed less sleep. Was this a common reaction to love?

Besides, what was love? Duke began typing a letter to Linda Lou on his word processor.

"You are the center of my universe. I hear your name in the wind; I see your face in my dreams." He stopped for a moment.

"I want to be with you every moment of the day," he continued typing. "You're more beautiful than the sunset."

Duke stopped typing and read what he had written. He punched the delete button. The screen went blank.

He felt like a fool writing a love letter. Why were men afraid to put their emotions on a blank piece of paper? Afraid of blackmail? Unmanly? Too open? Too exposed?

Duke had tried before to express his emotions to Linda Lou. He had folded several pieces of white paper and made a booklet. On the front he wrote "Top Secret." Inside he drew a funny face with the words "My heart beats for you." One sheet had a cut-out of Ben Franklin holding a kite string and said "Linda Lou is electrifying." He thought that was extremely witty. Another sheet had a clipping of two shoes and the statement "I would walk 100 miles for Linda Lou." He made little trails of red dots around the shoes. One of the trails of dots ended with the statement "I got lost here."

* * *

Moses had little time left in which to catch his plane. He put his luggage into his freshly battered vehicle and headed over to Hartsfield airport.

The only luggage he had was his Zenith laptop computer and a hanging bag. He carried these on the plane, and the flight was uneventful. His mind kept drifting to zombies, speeding cars, Ernie Anbert, and Kirby Forrest. "Were the obvious people the bad guys? Was it someone else? Would they try to kill again?"

Landing at National Airport was a little discomforting. The

runways at this older airport were shorter than most; consequently, the large passenger jets had to brake rather hard on landing. "The airport's convenient location was well worth this small price, though," Moses thought. It was always a little exhilarating to be in the hub of our nation's capitol.

Chapter 12

Government paperwork can be mind-boggling. The documents submitted by one company in its attempt to be selected to build the C5-A transport aircraft totaled 1,466,346 pages (a weight of almost 25,000 pounds).

Norman R. Ausgustine

Moses was soon checked into the Hyatt. After the plane ride, he felt the need to stretch and get some fresh air. Walking the Mall would be good exercise. Moses laughed to himself as he recalled a story about some tourists who thought that the Washington, D.C. Mall was an indoor shopping mall full of stores. In actuality, the Mall is a broad expanse of open land around which the most famous national monuments are situated. He took a taxi to the Capitol, which is at the east end of the Mall. He walked down the Capitol steps looking toward the Washington Monument which stood about a mile and half away in the center of the Mall. Beyond that tall monument, at the west end was the Lincoln Memorial. Close to the Lincoln Memorial was the Mall's more recent addition, the Vietnam Veterans' Memorial, referred to as "The Wall."

Moses could not resist a brief visit inside the Air and Space Museum, one of the 14 museums operated by the Smithsonian Institution. "Funny," he thought, "the Smithsonian was established by funds bequeathed to the U.S. by an Englishman, James Smithson. Little did that guy know what a famous American institution he would begin. Unlike Disneyland or Six Flags Over Georgia, admission is free."

Leaving the Air and Space Museum, he continued down the sidewalk alongside Jefferson Drive, passing the Smithsonian Castle which housed the Institution's first museum. The Castle is what comes to most people's minds when they think of the Smithsonian. Today it is primarily administrative offices.

Moses walked up the hill on which the Washington Monument stands. Flapping in the wind were the flags circling the monument. He could not resist the patriotic feeling that surged through him. In some small way he hoped that he made a contribution to the country's future welfare and prosperity. He participated in civic affairs. He never failed to vote. However, Moses was not one to urge everyone to vote. He thought that society would be better served if uninformed people stayed away from polling booths.

After resting a few minutes, he continued his long walk along the Mall, passing the large reflecting pools, to the Lincoln Memorial. Several times he caught a glimpse of his five foot eleven inch frame in the pool. He could see his short, brown hair, but not the few gray hairs that were peeping through. Inside the memorial, even though he had seen Lincoln's statue before, he gazed with awe. His hazel eyes read the words chiseled into the marble walls:

> ...Intelligence, patriotism, Christianity, and a firm reliance on Him who has never yet forsaken this favored land are still competent to adjust in the best way all our present difficulty... As was said three thousand years ago, so still it must be said, 'the judgments of the Lord are true and righteous altogether.'

"That war almost destroyed this country," thought Moses. "More Americans were killed in the Civil War than all the other wars combined." The sixteenth president had resolved not to allow the southern states to secede. At the Republican State Convention in Springfield, Illinois in June 1858, Abraham Lincoln quoted the Scripture that warned: "A house divided against itself cannot stand."

The institution of slavery was reluctantly accepted by the nation's founders as part of a political compromise enabling the thirteen former British colonies to join together to form the United States. The third president, Thomas Jefferson was deeply troubled by this political deal and admonished the nation with these words: "God who gave us life gave us liberty. Can the liberties of a nation be secure when we have removed a conviction that these liberties are the gift of God? Indeed I tremble for my country when I reflect that God is just, that his justice cannot sleep forever." More quotes from founding fathers are on the Web (http://acct.tamu.edu/smith/ethics/quotes.htm).

From the Lincoln Memorial, Moses walked over to the Vietnam Veteran's Memorial. "Another tragic war," he thought. On an earlier trip to Washington, he had found the names of several friends and relatives lost during that awful conflict. His eyes grew misty as he reflected on the tragic deaths of those men, literally cut down in their prime. He remembered General Sherman's assessment that war is hell. Wiping his eyes, he began his trek back to the Smithsonian Castle. There he would take the Metro, Washington's subway, to Crystal City where the Hyatt was located.

* * *

Moses awoke fresh the next morning. After a hearty breakfast, he entered the conference room on the second floor of the Hyatt. His session was for the purpose of discussing the current status of Russia's market system and the opportunities available to business persons. After introducing himself, he began his discussion.

"Let's begin by looking at the kind of market system, or lack of, under which the formerly Socialist economy of Russia operated. Years ago, Stalinist planners decided to build giant enterprises that concentrated production within a few outlets. Think of a few large corporations. In 1989, Russia had approximately 700,000 enterprises as compared to approximately 17 million in the United States. Each Russian enterprise was regulated by a government ministry. This ministry determined the needed labor and material inputs, while also setting production goals. The ministry determined the prices for the goods and the wages for labor. Most enterprises had an excess of labor in order to keep down unemployment. Regardless of whether Russian consumers bought the products, most of the industries were guaranteed to make a profit because the goods were sold to the ministry. There was no competition to stimulate improvements in product quality, no consumer research to determine what the consumer wanted, no profit incentive to determine the most efficient means of production or distribution, and no product research to develop new products. In other words, there was nothing marketing related, except for the selling of goods."

"Much of their retail trade took place in the factories and offices where people work, rather than in the stores. Along with paying wages, the government made businesses responsible for many aspects of their employees' lives. A host of in-plant goods and services were made available, such as clothing, delicatessens, consumer electronics, and dry cleaning. An employee ordered a new refrigerator through his place of business. Of course he'd be put on a waiting list for it."

Moses turned a page of his notes. "Russia has been characterized for its constant shortage of consumer goods, its sparsely stocked stores, and long waiting lines for the buyer. However, Russia actually produced an enormous abundance of goods. Year after year, Russia led in the production of things like oil, natural gas, iron ore, and steel. Goods often don't get to Russian consumers due to structural bottlenecks, particularly in the transport systems. The Russian economy relies heavily on its rail system which is plagued by problems. Imported goods often wind up sitting for weeks at ports while rail officials search desperately for trains to move them. Another problem is that the consumers refuse to buy certain products which are produced in their own country. They feel that the quality of Russian products is lower than similar products made in other countries."

"So what's the big picture here?" Moses asked the group.

"The consumer has very little choice over what she buys," a lady on the second row pointed out.

A young man commented, "Having your place of employment supply many of your needs offers security, yet what if you don't like what they supply. You've lost a lot of control over your personal life."

"If I knew the government was in charge of making everything, I wouldn't trust the quality of the products," another person commented. "I would rather buy imported things."

Moses responded, "That's exactly what one American businessman discovered. Russian consumers have a deep prejudice against many of the products manufactured in their country. Their personal preferences for certain product characteristics have been neglected for so long that they automatically assume products made in Russia will not be as good as products made elsewhere. Even when products are improved, this consumer attitude must be overcome. New Russian entrepreneurs will have to prove that their products are just as comfortable, or tasty, or long-lasting, or whatever."

Someone observed, "To whom do you complain if your new radio doesn't work or a shirt doesn't fit? It doesn't sound like the easy return policy of Wal-Mart is available over there!" The group chuckled.

A lady spoke up, "My kids have to keep five kinds of cereal constantly in stock; I think we Americans like variety, a luxury the Russians haven't had. We also like the ability to get what we want, when we want it. We complain if we have to wait ten minutes at the grocery store."

"All your comments," Moses explained, "are part of the reason Leonid Abalkin, a Russian Deputy Prime Minister for Economics, made the following statement: 'We have become convinced that there is no worthy alternative to the market mechanism.' He stated that there was no choice but to move toward a consistent denationalization of the entire Russian economy."

"When Mikhail Gorbachev came to power in 1985, he initiated perestroika, which is the restructuring of the former Soviet economy. The perception of economic stagnation had penetrated even the highest levels of their government. In 1987, Gorbachev pushed through some startling reforms, including new laws on joint ventures, cooperatives, and enterprise management. No longer were ministries to dictate labor input and production goals. Soviet industrial enterprises were made responsible for their own profits, products, and investments. It was a giant step toward turning the enterprises into full-fledged profit-oriented businesses."

"By abolishing the state's monopoly on foreign trade and legalizing foreign investment through the laws on joint ventures, Russian businessmen were given new economic freedom. They could seek foreign partners, trade abroad, and spend hard-currency profits without ministerial control. Of course, this didn't make everything a piece of cake. Business persons faced a new set of problems since they didn't know much about world markets and had almost no hard currency to use."

"One example of a product improvement was in the clothing industry. A Russian clothing factory bought Gerber Garment equipment for 2.5 million dollars and paid Gerber to train three Russian employees. The new equipment made it possible for the factory to create new styles of clothing in only 15 minutes. Previously, workers at the factory spent 16 days to accomplish this. Thus, the factory will be able to accommodate their consumers by reacting promptly to market and fashion changes."

A man in glasses commented, "American businesses seem to be taking the bait for joint ventures with the Russians. Moscow's McDonald's is a big success. It is the largest McDonald's restaurant in the world. They serve as many as 50,000 people a day. Pizza Hut, which is owned by Pepsi, is also in Moscow."

"I just read that Fiat has a plant there," a lady volunteered.

"Jeans are very popular in Russia,"a young man said with a smile. "Levi Strauss has a store in Moscow."

"Some Russian citizens don't know how to respond to the changing economy. The co-ops are still unpopular among the older and poorer citizens because of high prices and speculation. Businesses are caught part-way between the old command economy and a new one meant to respond to market signals and consumer demand. Inflation is part of the cost for having freed the large enterprises from the control of ministries and making them responsible for their own profits. They can raise prices, since there is an almost endless demand for their products. These enterprises currently dominate the market which has little, if any, competition. However, inflation isn't always overt since the government still has some price controls."

"Since the Russian newspapers have been liberated by glasnost (public openness or democratization), they print stories about the rising inflation rates and how people are reacting. A classic story is the great soap crises which occurred when Gorbachev's new economic ground rules came into play. Soapmakers switched to higher-cost brands of soap -- with higher profit margins. Out of habit, consumers began hoarding the lower-priced soaps, fearing an impending shortage. As a result, a shortage did occur and the consumers who couldn't get soap were quite upset! The government instituted rationing, co-ops sold soap at six times the regular price, striking miners made soap one of their demands, and doctors discovered patients whose apartments were so full of soap that they were suffering allergic reactions."

A lady raised her hand. "In your opinion Dr. McDonald, what is the biggest problem hindering a marketer in Russia?"

"That's a tough question. Certainly the worthlessness of their currency is a major impediment. Since the ruble is virtually worthless outside Russia, and almost worthless inside, a big problem is how to get profits out of the country. Even Russian taxi drivers have avoided rubles by requiring payment in cigarettes!"

"The trick for Western businessmen is to avoid spending hard currency for raw materials outside Russia when they have to sell the finished product inside for rubles. To avoid this trap. McDonald's buys all its beef, pickles, and buns for rubles in Russia."

Moses continued, "Since the ruble is so weak, companies are forced to rely on complicated countertrade deals to make money off their investments."

"Pepsi is an example of that," the Washingtonian pointed out. "Pepsi has been selling Stolichnaya vodka here in the States for hard currency to offset their soft drink sales in Russia. However, the vodka sales weren't keeping up with Pepsi's growth over there, so Pepsi signed a new deal to trade Pepsi-Colas, pizzas, and Kentucky Fried Chicken for 85 ships worth nearly 2.6 billion dollars. They then sell the ships to Western shipping firms at a profit."

Moses advised, "Even barter deals are getting harder to negotiate. There's a limited number of products one would wish to trade for, and many of these have already been taken. Some products offered by the Russians are World War II submarines, which could be used for scrap metal, and field mouse skins, which could be used for wallets!"

Another woman commented, "I knew their government was

desperate for foreign currency when they were willing to sell commercial sponsorship of one of their space missions. The deal included billboards at the launch site and the sponsor's decal on the spaceship!" Moses considered that remark for a moment. In his mind's eye he pictured the U.S. space shuttle with a Coke logo painted on the side.

"The currency problem may be easier to change, however, than human attitudes," Moses said. "Many Western business people have given up when faced with the long-entrenched centralized bureaucracy of Russians. Although a new course had been set for their market system, actual change is a slow process. You must remember that we're dealing with a culture that has been strongly resistant to capitalistic ideas."

"Of course, there's lots of other obstacles for a marketer to overcome in Russia. There's high tax rates, unreliable sources of supply, worker alienation, out-dated technology, and inadequate communication systems. I know of a company that's been operating a new factory over there for ten months now and they've only been able to get one phone hooked up! All these impediments definitely detract from the attractiveness of lower wage rates and eager consumers."

Moses posed a new way of looking at the issue. "Rather than asking what products, the more important question may be: who are the companies that can make a go of it? Since it will probably take a decade to realize any return on an investment, the corporate powerhouses are the ones that should break into the Russian market. Their motivation for doing so now, instead of waiting a few years, is the Japanese and European competition. There's a market of 287 million people sitting atop enormous natural resources and anxious for foreign products. As the Russian economy slowly rejoins the world, the Russian consumer will not stay poor forever."

"If you don't want to wait for your profit, your best bet is to set up a business that caters to foreign businessmen. These customers have hard currency! The business could house, feed, transport, or advise. For example, an Atlanta real estate firm, the Worsham Group, is aiding Moscow's city council in converting old buildings to modern offices. Foreigners are so desperate for office space in Moscow that square footage cost is very expensive. A basement suite may go for $110 per square foot a month."

"Dr. McDonald, what advice would you give the Russian leaders?"

"I believe that a page of history is worth a volume of logic. I see an analogy between Japan and Russia. Not many years ago Japan suffered an image of poor quality. At one time the phrase 'made in Japan' meant poor quality. How did Japan overcome this image problem?"

Moses looked around the room. "They radically improved the quality of their goods. They now have only 200 rejects for each million units. The U.S. has 50,000 rejects per million units. The Japanese have almost totally eliminated mistakes. As the number of mistakes went down, productivity went up, and now they dominate. 'Made in Japan' now means excellent craftsmanship. That is what Russia must do. That is what the U.S. or any country must do. Quality control is essential."

Moses gathered his lecture notes and said, "To sum up Russia's potential, it's a market for big companies with deep pockets and long-sighted visions."

"Well, I see it's time for this morning session to end. I've covered as much as I could during my allotted time period. I hope it was beneficial to all of you. For those of you who aren't going to another session right away, I'll be around if you have any further questions." The audience began clapping. Moses turned red from embarrassment.

After the conference, Moses checked out of his hotel and took a shuttle bus to National Airport. He was anxious to get back to Atlanta. His daughter, Katie, would be waiting at home to greet him along with his unsolved case.

Upon returning, Katie expressed her relieve to have Moses back safe and sound. Moses didn't tell his daughter that's exactly how he feels every time she comes in the door. After settling into bed later that night, his mind drifted to the Coke audit. He realized that tomorrow was the day Duke and Linda would leave for Poland. Moses hoped the two of them would have a pleasant trip together. "Romance is in the air," he thought before drifting off to sleep. "Maybe I can find the smoking gun while he's gone. Ernie Anbert? Kirby Forrest? Both? Someone else?"

The next morning at work, Moses decided to ask Chuck Morgan about Kirby Forrest.

"Sure I know him," Chuck began. "He was the resident computer nut when I started working at Coke. He retired just a few months ago."

"What do you know about him?" Moses asked.

"Not much really. He seemed to be a very refined, older gentleman. But not stuffy. Very friendly. I had to get his help with some computer problems a few times. Unlike some computer experts I know, Kirby spoke plain English, not computer jargon. He really knew his stuff. He could explain things so that anyone could understand. You know I really hate it when anyone tells me that some so-called expert knows his stuff, but just can't explain it to others. Heck, that expert doesn't know his stuff. He's just faking it!"

"Whoa, buddy. You're getting on one of your soapboxes. Let's get back to the subject. You remember, Kirby Forrest? Do you know what he's doing now?"

"Well, I heard that he's seeing the world. He sends postcards back to the old gang here at Coke. We post them on the bulletin board in the coffee room. The last one is still up, some place in Pakistan. No, India, I think. He may be back home by now. Why are you so interested in Kirby? Some question about the computer system?"

"Yeah, basically that's it. I'll tell you all about it later." Moses started to leave Morgan's office.

"Hold on, Moses. I just remembered something. When Linda first came to Coke, she worked a lot with Kirby in restructuring marketing files. She could probably tell you more about him."

Moses scratched his head. "That's a big help, Chuck. I'll check with her when she gets back from overseas. Thanks for the info." Moses turned and left Morgan's office.

he walked toward his office, Moses mused over his information. "This is great! If Kirby Forrest is the culprit, then Linda may be able to help us figure out exactly what he did. Meanwhile, if Forrest has returned from his travels, I'll get the spy equipment Duke purchased and see if I can pick up any computer signals from outside his home. This caper is getting too interesting to wait 'til Duke and Linda return."

Chapter 13

Successful marketing begins with understanding why and how consumers behave. Example: Campbell's Soup, Procter & Gamble, and Metropolitan Life Insurance tailor their products, advertising, and sales efforts to fit the unique needs of various regional, ethnic, and racial subcultures in the U.S.

Eric Berkowitz, Roger Kerin, and William Rudelius

After a short fuel break in Paris, their Pan Am 747 flight landed at Tegel Airport in West Berlin. Duke and Linda collected their suitcases and rented a blue Ford. Duke had a difficult time getting Linda Lou's large suitcases in the trunk. Soon they drove southwest toward the center of the city.

"We still have some time before dusk. I'll take you to see remnants of the 'wall.' The best viewing spot is at Potsdamer Platz," Linda said. "Coca-Cola's initial move to create goodwill with consumers in what used to be East Germany occurred when the wall first came down. They offered free Cokes to people crossing the border."

"Some parts of the wall still stand. It once snaked across the city, splitting Berlin in half. After the Potsdam Treaty on August 2, 1945, the city of Berlin was governed by a Four Powers Agreement. East Berlin was controlled by Russia. West Berlin was divided into the American, British, and French zones. The Wall appeared overnight on August 13, 1961, to prevent immigration from East to West Berlin. At first, the wall was just miles of jagged barbed wire. But soon the barbed wire was replaced with a concrete wall, rising ten to thirteen feet tall. It became the coldest symbol of a divided Europe."

"The 860 mile long wall was really two walls with a no-man's-land between the two. In the middle was the killing zone--land mines, attack dogs, and self-triggering shotguns. Occasionally, along the route, stood a watch tower with two soldiers. A bonus was paid for any person the guards stopped--dead or alive. The guards were never put on duty twice together to avoid the development of a friendship.

Two friendly guards might have escaped together."

"Then, beginning in the fall of 1989, the wall was dismantled and the communist government allowed its citizens the freedom to travel. Civil unrest in East Germany and other communist countries pressured their leaders to ease up travel restrictions. Political reform began taking place throughout Eastern Europe.

At Potsdamer Platz, Linda and Duke scrambled up a platform to look at the former East German zone. Pointing to the desolate land between the two sectors of Berlin, Linda said, "See that small mound of dirt? That's the air raid shelter where Hitler committed suicide in 1945."

"I read that at least three-and one-half million Germans fled from the East to the West before the Wall was built in 1961. That was a big brain drain," Duke interjected. "After the wall was dismantled in 1989, some people left East Germany, but the overwhelming majority stayed in their native country with the hope that the new freedoms would remain in effect. As it turned out their hopes were fulfilled when Germany was reunified."

"Checkpoint Charlie, the famed allied border crossing between East and West, went up with the Berlin Wall in 1961. It was taken down shortly after the wall was dismantled," Duke continued. "It was quite an elaborate ceremony with a brass band, foreign ministers from Germany and the four allies, a mess of generals, and hundreds of reporters. Oddly, the public wasn't invited!"

An older German lady standing close by told them, "I use to live just a few yards from Checkpoint Charlie, in an upstairs apartment. I could see the checkpoint from my window."

Interested, Duke asked, "Did you ever see anyone escape?"

The lady smiled, "I saw several escapes. Some were in customized vehicles, some came through a tunnel across the street, and some would walk very slowly, look around and then run as fast as they could."

Her smile then disappeared as she sadly recalled, "I also saw people shot to death in their attempt to escape."

Linda sighed. "I'm impressed by the Berliners' attitude."

Looking at a preserved section of the wall, she said, "Apparently most of the wall was painted in this colorful graffiti. I saw another section of the wall at the George Bush Presidential Library at Texas A&M University. It also had colorful graffiti which expressed the hope which remained alive in the spirits of the people."

"Let's get a picture of the Wall." Duke climbed down from the platform and walked over to the concrete demarcation line. He pretended to be climbing the symbol of oppression.

Linda snapped a shot of him. The Wall looked to be about twelve feet tall.

After saying good-bye to their German acquaintance, they got back in their car. Linda said, "You know that some entrepreneurs actually sold authentic parts from the Berlin wall. A small piece taken directly from the wall was sold in a soft pouch inside a cardboard box, with a booklet about the wall, and a declaration of authenticity and origin. It sold for as high as $15. Good, timely marketing. Someone gave me one of those historic artifacts." Linda laughed.

"Sure, Linda Lou, I bet you bought it yourself," Duke quipped.

With Duke driving, they passed the Brandenburg Gate, the entrance to the city. This majestic archway was once closed since it is flush with what was once the oppressive Berlin Wall. Linda pointed to the infamous Checkpoint Charlie. "They used to push wheeled mirrors under every vehicle to see if anyone was clinging to the bottom. That's how desperate people were to escape communism."

"You know, nearly every communist country has shifted away from total state control of its economy and moved toward a market economy that permits some free enterprise activity. It's amazing how things have changed," Duke marveled.

"From a marketer's point of view, one which I often take," Linda chuckled, "Eastern Europe represents millions of consumers who are craving for products. In the past few years, Eastern European countries have installed more liberal laws in order to encourage joint ventures between foreign and local investors. One incentive is tax reductions to joint ventures with Western partners."

Duke nodded in agreement. "I've read that a joint venture with an Eastern European partner is a good way for a Western investor to break into the market. One does a lot of reading in graduate school, you know." Duke paused, looked toward Linda, then back toward the road. "The Eastern partner can stay in touch with rapidly changing local conditions, plus risk is reduced since it is shared."

"From a risk standpoint, do you think a partnership or a corporation is more conservative?" Linda asked.

"Well, partners share the profits but they also share the legal liability for any debts incurred by the enterprise. That's why a corporation instead of a partnership is more attractive to me. In a corporation, stockholders are the legal owners with rights to the profits, but their legal liability is limited. The stockholders cannot be sued for failure of the corporation to pay its debts; only the corporation itself can be sued."

"American companies have only a small share of the consumer product market in Eastern Europe," Linda mused. " Of course, there are difficulties and frustrations in dealing with the East European market. These countries are still highly volatile politically and economically. The Eastern European governments love it if the Western partner brings in hard currency. There are restrictions on hard currency transactions. The catch comes when it's time to convert profits from the host-country currency to hard currency. The exchange rate may be controlled by the government. This control is a crucial issue for the Western investor when he wants to convert his profits into dollars and bring the money home. An agreement regarding repatriation can be negotiated with the host government, but there is no guarantee that future government officials of a formerly communist country will keep the agreement. It may be possible to acquire insurance against losses resulting from government trade restrictions or against other hazards such as strikes, riots, or expropriation. Besides using private insurance companies, the U.S. Overseas Private Investment Corporation and the Export-Import Bank can help in some countries."

After checking into their hotel, Linda and Duke walked to the Victory Tower. Along the way the trees were green and the flowers were blooming. They passed a park and smiled at some bizarre dressed young people enjoying the wonderful weather.

The Victory Tower celebrates the end of the Franco-Prussian War. They climbed the 285 steps to the top--slowly. There was a great view of the entire city and the Brandenberg Bridge. Linda and Duke enjoyed some lingering kisses at the top of the tower -- standing next to the angel on top.

While looking toward the eastern portion of the city, Linda pointed and said, "Do you see that television tower? It is almost 1,200 feet high and the top has a revolving restaurant. When the sun shines on the restaurant, sometimes a cross appears on it. West Berliners named the tower the Pope's Revenge." She leaned over and snuggled against Duke, amidst the noise of the street traffic below.

Duke was enjoying himself. Coca-Cola's problems were far removed from his mind.

After more sight-seeing, the couple returned to their hotel. Their hotel rooms were so small that Duke had to remove a chair from Linda's room in order to make space for her suitcases.

The next morning, because of jet lag, Duke awoke at 3:30.Duke and Linda met for breakfast at six o'clock. Afterwards, they loaded into their rental car and started the drive to Poland. As they drove out of Berlin, they stopped at the 1936 Olympic Stadium. Jesse Owens won his gold medals here. "Der Fuhrer" really fumed when Owens triumphed over members of his "master race" four times. The lush green field was now used mostly for soccer.

By 10:20 they reached the former East German border. Soon they were traveling across what had been East Germany.

Linda thought about the inroads Coke was making in the German soft-drink market. "Coke spent 140 million dollars in capital investments to upgrade bottling plants. Negotiations were started with beverage organizations soon after the wall came down. Coke was able to break into this market fairly easily because the former East Germans already knew about Coca-Cola; they had been seeing television ads from the West for 30 years. Plus, the existence of bottling facilities in what had been West Germany allowed Coke to expand operations quickly in the unified country."

"There are some fast-growing market segments, including diet soft drinks and vending machines, that are still in an infant stage here," Linda Lou commented. "There's so much growth potential here. While the U.S. soft-drink volume has slowed to about a three percent annual growth rate, the international market is expected to grow in nine percent leaps annually for years to come."

"In how many countries is Coke?" asked Duke.

"Coke is in over 160 countries, including the former Soviet Union, China, and some of the countries here around us -- Czechoslovakia, Bulgaria, Hungary, Poland, and Yugoslavia. Coke is one of the world's most popular and best recognized consumer products. Its advertising looks the same all over the world. Coke's philosophy is 'one sight, one sound, one sell.' Of course the ads must be adapted to varying cultural values and differences."

"It sounds like Coke dominates the international soft-drink market," Duke surmised.

"Coke has about half of the international market share. In an effort to close the gap against Coke internationally, Pepsi has a plan to spend one billion dollars to improve marketing programs, distribution, and plants. They think this marketing program will double their international soft drink sales. Pepsi is trying to catch up, but of course I don't think they can," boasted Linda.

"The name of the game is consolidation of resources. By consolidating plants, distribution systems, sales forces, and accounting systems--we can exploit economies of scale."

"So, Linda Lou, refresh my memory on what your primary mission is on this trip?" Duke asked with interest. "I've been a bit distracted lately."

"We need to build a 'super plant' in order to spread our total costs over the largest feasible number of units. Total cost is made up of two things: total fixed cost plus total variable cost. I probably need to refresh your memory on basic accounting facts," Linda said with a grin. "You've had your head stuck in a computer so long! Variable cost varies directly with output, increasing as more output is produced.

However, fixed cost does not vary, at least in the short run. Thus, the more we can produce, the lower our average fixed cost per unit will be. Average total cost is equal to the total cost of production divided by the number of units of output."

"Of course, economies and diseconomies of scale play a part in how big the plant will be. Economies of scale can be achieved through more efficient use of equipment, specialized jobs, quantity discounts in purchasing, and even getting a better economic package from the host community. As the plant size and output increases, average total cost falls. This occurs until bigness starts becoming costly. Further growth then causes average total cost to rise and results in diseconomies of scale. Diseconomies result primarily from the fact that as an organization becomes very large, communication, coordination, and control become more difficult and time-consuming, and thus inefficient."

"Did I get carried away?" Linda asked innocently. "Anyway, I'll be part of a negotiation team to discuss placing a super bottling plant in Poland. We'll be in meetings for the next two days. The guidelines on ownership of capital ventures vary greatly in Europe. Poland allows up to fifty percent foreign ownership without government permission and higher percentages if the government approves. We hope to get the approval for a higher percentage. Most countries require a minimum capital contribution if foreign ownership is permitted." Linda paused, then smiled. "As you may know, Poland has the highest birth rate in Europe. I read in some underground literature that reproduction in Poland is an undercover activity." Linda laughed and said, "Maybe it was a Solidarity slogan."

"Where will the plant be located?" asked Duke.

"Hopefully east of Krakow, near a small town called Oswiecim. It's almost in the center of Europe with railroad tracks leading like spokes throughout Europe."

"Oswiecim. Have I heard that name before?"

"Possibly," Linda nodded. "That's where the Nazis' concentration camp, Auschwitz, was located. Between 1940 and 1945 more than four million, mainly Jewish, prisoners were gassed or shot by the Nazis and then burned. Of course, you can recognize our public relations problem. We'll have to create another small town near Auschwitz to avoid a possible negative public reaction. Hitler selected Oswiecim because of its central location."

"Isn't there an alternate location?" Duke asked.

"Yes. Near Czestochowa. That's the location of a Pauline monastery which houses the most revered religious shrine in the country--The Black Madonna. Whatever location is ultimately selected, the super plant must be on rail spurs in order to reduce shipping costs."

"Some dilemma," said Duke. "Should Coke pick the best location which is at the site of the Nazis' appalling inhumanity to mankind or pick the lesser location at the center of Polish religious and cultural life? Should you optimize or satisfice?"

"What?"

"Should you optimize by seeking the largest payoff, or should you satisfice by pursuing an 'acceptable' rather than an optimal decision? What spot would the Pope pick?"

"Hey, just south of Oswiecim is Wadowice, the birthplace of Pope John Paul II," quipped Linda. "Actually, we're in the process of developing criteria for 'acceptability' by reviewing what happened in other organizations, what Coke's past track record is, and what people will accept. We're also computing the explicit cost (the money outlay) for each location. Another consideration is the implicit cost, which is the cost implied by the alternatives given up. In other words, the opportunity cost of production."

"Is there anything about this bottling plant to interest a computer maniac like me?"

Linda smiled. "The production facility will be controlled by a black box data processing system. The big computer will run eight to ten lines at high speed. We are talking about 1,600 to 2,000 containers per minute."

"What did Churchill say? Never has so much been delivered to so many by so few." After a few moments Duke continued. "I thought there was an embargo of high-tech computers to communist countries."

"An astute observation!" responded Linda. "That's why we're meeting with Janusz Reykowski tomorrow. He's the same person who negotiated the political agreement with Solidarity in 1989. We must negotiate some type of business agreement to assure the State Department that the big computer will not get into the hands of Polish military. There's a lot of money made in Poland by circumventing the computer embargo."

At Frankfurt-on-the-Oder they crossed the Oder River to go to Poland. They stopped and their passports and visas were checked by a Polish border guard. They filled out a declaration form indicating how much money they were carrying into Poland. Any currency in excess of what is entered on the form is subject to confiscation. Also, travelers to Poland must exchange a minimum of $15 per day at the official exchange rate.

Poland, thanks to almost 50 years of Soviet-enforced Marxism-Leninism, became one of the poorest of the Eastern bloc countries. Unstable, with a steadily deteriorating quality of life, its 37 million inhabitants lived a grim daily existence. However, even under communist rule, its citizens remained devoutly religious. The Catholic Church is an important force, with more than 90 percent of the people Roman Catholics. Even communist oppression could not eradicate Christianity. For that matter, neither could Roman oppression two thousand years earlier.

The main road ran across a flat terrain and was in poor condition. Linda and Duke turned onto a minor road leading to a small town named Rezipen. The minor road was narrow and the travelers had to frequently slow for horse drawn carts. They noticed many horses being used in the fields, and the land-owners using sickles to cut their crops.

Rezipen was a little town of about 15,000 people. A quaint, little restaurant served an enjoyable lunch. They started with an appetizer of baked chicken, followed with a bowl of potato soup with mushroom, a cucumber salad, and sliced tomato. Then came the pork chops, gravy, potatoes, custard, coke, and vodka.

"Some lunch," said Duke outside the restaurant.

"You understand, Duke, that food supplies are erratic in Poland,"

Linda said. "A housewife may spend hours each day in a long line trying to buy food for her family."

Linda saw a little girl sitting on the steps next door to the restaurant. She took her picture, and then gave her a 20 zoltys coin. The little girl beamed.

Since Warsaw was about 320 miles from the German border, it was about 7:30 when they arrived at the Forum Hotel in Warsaw, the capital of Poland. As they were checking into the hotel, the hotel clerk stamped their visas. Tourists are required to have a stamp on their visas indicating where they've slept each night.

After getting their luggage to their rooms, they took a cab to the Old Market restaurant called Kamienne Schodki. Tucked away at the corner of the Old Market, stone stairs descend to the Vistula River which bisects Warsaw.

While waiting for their roast duck, Linda Lou gave Duke a short history of Warsaw. "Poland was the first country attacked by Nazi Germany in 1939. No other city suffered more than Warsaw during WWII. Hitler gave orders to destroy Warsaw. There were four weeks of bombing, and then the German soldiers razed the city to the ground. Nothing was left in the systematic destruction, except 45,000 corpses under the ruins. Everything, with clinical precision, was destroyed with dynamite and petrol. When the army of liberation entered Warsaw in January 1945, not a single human being lived there. Even Hiroshima had some survivors. What had taken 700 years to build, the Germans wiped out in less than two months."

"Like a phoenix rising from its ashes," Linda continued, "the Polish people rebuilt the city. This Old Town district was rebuilt exactly as it was before the destruction. The architects used paintings, old prints, and family photographs to rebuild 18th century buildings in this area. You noticed that Old Town is closed to all traffic except horse-drawn cabs."

"Poland is flat, but those large hills we saw as we entered Warsaw are large mounds of the debris carried from the destroyed city. Every citizen became a builder, and a new city came to life."

Duke decided to change the course of conversation. "Linda,

what's your favorite movie?" he asked.

"That's hard to say," she replied. "Name a category."

"Okay. The category is science fiction."

"Easy. My favorite science fiction movie is Forbidden Planet," Linda responded.

Duke thought for a moment. "That's a classic for sure," he said. "I really liked Robbie the Robot. My favorite sci-fi flick, however, is the Star Wars saga."

"Now that you mention it, you remind me a little of Han Solo." Linda said with a flirtatious grin.

"Okay, new category -- adventure." Duke stated with gusto.

Linda thought for a moment, then said, "Robin Hood, starring Kevin Costner. That movie was also romantic." She sighed. "I like romance and adventure. You can't have one without the other."

"I wouldn't have it any other way." Duke smiled. "Robin Hood also had some great scenes involving archery. Bows and arrows are ancient but very effective weapons."

Linda pantomimed holding a bow and aiming an arrow at Duke.

Duke grinned. "Watch where you point that thing." He pretended to be hit by an arrow.

Linda added to the drama. "We few, we happy few, we band of brothers; for he today that sheds his blood with me shall be my brother."

"That sounds familiar." Duke tried to recall where he had heard that.

"Let me ease that crinkled brow of yours," Linda said lightheartedly. "It's from Shakespeare's Henry the Fifth. It's part of the speech that King Henry gave his troops just before the battle of Agincourt. The battle where 45,000 Frenchmen were defeated by only 7,000 English archers."

"I'm impressed," Duke admitted.

Just then, the waiter arrived with their meal. While eating, Duke and Linda expanded their conversation to include books, hobbies, and their philosophies about life. Each was amazed at how much they thought alike.

After the tasty roast duck, the waiter brought the bill of 620 zoltys, under $4.00 based upon the official rate of exchange. Linda whispered to the waiter, "Will you exchange U.S. dollars?"

"How much?" the waiter asked patiently.

"$40.00," she whispered back.

"No problem," replied the smiling waiter.

"What rate?" asked Linda.

"Twice the official rate."

"I can get that with travelers checks. Give me three times the official rate."

"No way. I'll give two and one-half. No more," the waiter replied indignantly.

"Okay," she replied, "How?"

"Put the $40 under the napkin, under your bill. I'll take out 620 zoltys, and I'll give you the difference."

Linda followed the instructions.

Shortly the waiter returned and left the plate with the zoltys on the table. Linda took the money and left a 400 zoltys tip. Duke was uneasy watching her trade through the black market. However, he knew this was not the place to discuss it.

Outside, blue-jeaned pedestrians still filled the street and a white-coated soda water ("woda sodowa") vendor stood by his parasoled cart. Duke saw a hot dog vendor fill a roll with dollops of stewed mushrooms from his trailer. He handed the hot dog to a young man dressed in a U.S. Army style jacket.

After a short cab ride back to the Forum and inside her room, Linda counted her money. She then asked Duke, "What's the official exchange rate?"

"About 165 zoltys per one dollar."

"Not bad. I beat the 'official' rate by over 15,000 zoltys. But the real black-market or parallel rate is about four times the official rate."

"You do know it's illegal to exchange money in the black-market. It's dangerous," Duke warned. "The state still has the power of capricious arrest and a long detention without trial."

* * *

For the next two days, Linda was part of the Coca-Cola team involved in a number of meetings with bottling personnel, Polish governmental officials, and various consultants. Problems confronting a foreign investor include government regulations, trade barriers, and foreign corruption. Coke's particular dilemmas were numerous:

1. Pros and cons of the two plant locations--Oswiecim or Czestochowa.
2. Ways for Coca-Cola to remove any profits from Poland. Importing and exporting Polish currency is not permitted.
3. The percentage ownership of the participants, Coca-Cola and Poland, in the joint venture.
4. The amount each participant will provide the joint venture.
5. The control of the "super computer" by Coca-Cola in order to convince U.S. officials to approve export of such a powerful computer to Poland.

Janusz Reykowski attended one of the meetings and did not look like the bad guy Linda had envisioned. Reykowski indicated that he hoped to solve his country's economic and social problems with his free-market economy. But even in his dark-blue suit and red necktie, his ramrod-straight military attitude surfaced when he insisted that the joint venture could take profits out of Poland only if the venture generated hard-currency earnings.

At the end of the first day, Linda had more a sense of frustration than accomplishment. "Doing business here is certainly different than in the States," she complained to Duke. "Quality control is naturally poor here since businesses haven't been challenged by competition for the past forty years. They don't understand the profit motive very well. Communications are difficult using the existing inadequate telephone system. The labor market is chaotic and productivity is low. Supply channels are unreliable. Shall I go on? Of course these aren't pressing problems like the question over property ownership. Much of the land is currently state-owned. While private ownership is likely to be restored, it will take years. Meanwhile, there is much debate over who controls the property. I hope tomorrow goes better."

At the end of the second day of negotiations, things were looking much brighter to Linda. The Polish government and Coca-Cola issued the following agreement which appeared later in *Poityka*, a weekly journal:

> Coca-Cola and Poland have reached a tentative agreement to build a "super" bottling plant in Poland. The location of the plant is still under consideration. Coca-Cola, with a 51 percent stake, will control the joint venture.
>
> A state-of-the-art data processing system will control nine lines at high speeds, to produce 1,800 containers per minute. The profit distributable by the joint venture shall be the excess of its net profit over income tax payable and the required provisions of reserve fund, staff and worker's bonus and welfare fund, and enterprise expansion fund. It shall be distributed to the participants of the joint venture in proportion to their shares of contributed capital. The restrictions on currency transactions are being discussed.
>
> Coca-Cola will retain control over technology transfers. Imports and exports will be under Coca-Cola's jurisdiction. The labor force will be comprised of local people. Some personnel will come from the U.S.
>
> The assets of the joint venture left over after the clearance of all its debts shall be distributed among the participants of the joint venture according to the proportion of each participant's investment contribution, unless otherwise provided by the agreement, contract, or articles of association of the joint venture.

Duke did not attend the two days of meetings, but instead checked on the sales accounts of the major Polish Coca-Cola bottler. He knew that computer systems did not eliminate the need for old fashioned fact checking. In the evening, over dinner, he told Linda Lou, "Look, information from a computer data bank is only as good as the person who typed in the original information. I found a good example of this today. I noticed unexplainable swings in sales transactions reported in certain branches. I finally traced the discrepancies to a clerk who occasionally added four zeros to actual figures to ease boredom."

"At the bottler's headquarters, there was an internal control procedure in which two clerks were required to verify the quantity, price, and extension of sales transactions. They initialed the duplicate sales invoice to indicate performance. To verify the control's effectiveness, I examined a sample of the duplicate sales invoices for the initials of the two workers who verified the quantitative data. I found that there were a significant number of documents without initials. I extended my test of the duplicate sales invoices by verifying prices, extensions, and footings. The findings revealed that the invoices were correct, because the original clerks preparing the sales invoices had done competent jobs."

The next morning Linda was busy at work. Duke had completed his investigations and had some free time. Consequently, he decided to visit a local museum. He had seen a roadside sign for the museum when he and Linda first arrived into town. Duke thought that visiting a museum was almost as exciting and adventuresome as a trip in a time machine. Museums made history three-dimensional. Exploring a museum was like a mysterious adventure.

On the drive to the museum he made a few wrong turns but eventually found his way. Reading roadmaps was not his forte' in the States, let along in a foreign country. When he did finally arrive at the museum parking lot, he noted that there were only a couple of other cars present. "Drat, it's probably closed," he grumbled to himself. As he pulled into a parking space, he saw a sign on the large wooden entrance door indicating the museum hours. "Hmmm. Well, the sign says this is visiting hours." He turned off the ignition.

Duke left his car and headed toward the building's entrance which was about 20 yards away. Just as he pulled open the heavy door, he thought he heard another car drive up. He started to turn and look at the other tourists. Before he could look, his attention was redirected by a friendly greeting from an elderly lady sitting at a desk just inside the doorway. He smiled in return. Her initial greeting had been in Polish but she quickly discerned that the tall young man was an American and said with only a slight accent, "Hello and welcome. Five dollars, U.S., to visit our museum."

Duke reached for his wallet. As he did so, he scanned his surroundings. He was in a small lobby area. He observed a rack of postcards and the usual assortment of souvenirs for sale. He extracted a five dollar bill from his wallet and handed it to the lady. She told him that he could follow signs for a self-directed tour around the museum but that if he came back later that day a tour guide would be available.

"Well, I like to go at my own pace anyway, so I'll pass on the tour guide, ma'am," Duke politely said.

"That is fine," she responded. "This is the best museum in Poland and you have picked an excellent day to visit us," she added. "Only yesterday we finished setting up a new display on medieval warfare in the south wing. You will enjoy that, I think. Most of our paintings are located in the north wing, but there are many scattered throughout the museum." She paused, then continued, "Also, you simply must visit our exhibits on the second floor above the north wing. We have dedicated that area to the Second World War and its aftermath. I hope you enjoy your visit."

"Thank you very much," Duke said. He hoped the museum was worthy of such praise. If it was, he was about to have some serious fun. He turned with a smile and headed toward the arched doorway located on the other side of the room. A sign above the doorway had a message in Polish, German, and English. The English message stated "Central Corridor."

Walking through the doorway, Duke was amazed at the length of the hall before him. On the left and right of the hall were entrances to small rooms which contained various exhibits. Before stopping to examine anything in detail, he decided to walk all the way to the end of the hall and get a general feel for the museum's layout. As he walked the lengthy central corridor, Duke was initially impressed by two things, lofty ceilings and a musty odor. Each exhibit room he passed was packed with various objects and artifacts. He was tempted to stop at a couple of exhibits but kept walking until he was about halfway down the hall. Here was an intersection of two halls. He could go left, right, or straight ahead. A sign above the left entranceway indicated that was the way to the north wing; and a sign above the right, to the south wing. Remembering the attendant's recommendation, he decided to visit the medieval warfare display in the south wing.

Turning to his right, he was suddenly impressed with the many paintings, tapestries, and displays hanging from the walls. Everything seemed ancient, yet well preserved. Duke surmised the museum was laid out along two long hallways, each bisecting the other, forming a cross. When he reached the end of the south wing, Duke entered the last exhibit room on the right. He was awestruck by a spectacular painting that took up most of the wall across the room from the entrance. The painting was extremely lifelike and depicted a medieval castle under siege.

A huge ballista firing large spears toward the castle stood in the foreground of the painting. Two siege towers stood against the castle walls. The attacking troops were swarming up the towers and onto the adjoining castle walls. Soldiers fighting on both sides of the battle were hard at work with swords, axes, halberds, maces, lances, as well as longbows and crossbows. Archers had filled the air with arrows. The attacking troops seemed to have the upper hand.

Duke was drawn into the room by the painting. As he stepped inside, he noticed an assortment of medieval weapons on display. Standing on each side of the entrance was a rack containing three crossbows. The ancient crossbow was an extremely effective weapon which consisted of a bow set transversely on a wooden stock. The stock, was grooved to direct the projectile and notched to hold the bowstring. After the bowstring was drawn up, a trigger released it. Thus, the crossbowman could take aim without having to maintain the effort of holding the bowstring back. Unlike the long arrows used with a regular bow, a crossbow used either a short arrow called a bolt or simply a stone.

Next to each crossbow rack was a stand of about a dozen lances. Lances were used by footsoldiers as well as mounted troops. In his mind, Duke pictured two knights on horseback charging each other, lances aiming for their opponent.

Duke walked past the lances to a display of swords. He was particularly impressed with a large two-handed sword. Brute strength was evidently necessary to wield such a weapon in an efficient and effective manner. In the display with the swords, he noticed a massive battle ax. The ax was double-sided and the blade on each side was notched in several places. Apparently, the ax had seen service in some long-ago time and place, perhaps in an event much like that shown in the painting. He wondered how long he would have survived on that ancient battlefield.

Duke proceeded toward the painting. One final display held shields made of thick wood and reinforced with iron strips. One shield was painted with a coat of arms. The coat of arms featured a griffin, a mythical animal with the body and hind legs of a lion, and the head and wings of an eagle. Turning away from the shields, he discovered he was only a few feet from the large painting. All the time Duke had been in the museum, he had seen no one except the attendant. Yet, as he stood gazing at the painting he had an inexplicable feeling that he was being observed. Duke turned toward the entrance to the room. Something was different but what he couldn't say. He then realized how eerily quiet the museum was. Next, he shook his head, and mumbled to himself, "Must be ghosts." He chuckled and turned back toward the painting.

Duke heard a loud twang. Instantly he was jerked from his feet and slammed into the painting and the stone wall behind it. He grunted loudly on impact. He grimaced at the sharp pain in his left shoulder, the first part of his body to hit the wall. He started to turn toward the room's entrance but was able to turn only part way around. Standing in the entrance was a darkly dressed person holding a crossbow. Duke then realized what had been out of place, a crossbow had been removed from a rack by the room's entrance. Uttering a barely audible curse, the assailant tossed the weapon to the floor. In the next second, the assailant grabbed another crossbow from the rack and began to pull back the drawstring. At the same time Duke tried to move but was firmly pinned against the painting. He looked at his shoulder and saw a feathered shaft protruding from near the top of his coat sleeve. He was momentarily panicked at the thought of being badly wounded. Gathering his wits, he realized that although his arm hurt, it didn't hurt that bad. The crossbow bolt had merely caught the edge of his coat sleeve, completely missing his arm. Nevertheless, he was in a precarious situation.

Duke looked again toward the entrance. The attacker was still at work arming the weapon. Cocking the crossbow required the bowman to kneel and to hold the weapon vertically, front against the ground. By leaning forward over the crossbow and placing a shoulder against the base of the stock, both hands could be used to pull back the bowstring. As Duke watched, the attacker stood upright and fitted a bolt in front of the drawn bowstring.

"I'm about to die, for real this time!" Duke thought. He pulled with all his might but didn't budge. Apparently his coat was made of a fine quality fabric, not easily ripped. Heart racing, adrenalin pumping, Duke wrestled his arms out of the coat, leaving it hanging as if part of the painting display. In his rush to free himself, he lost his balance and stumbled into the shield display. This may have saved his life. He grabbed the shield with the griffin's picture and held it between him and the attacker. He heard a loud metallic "thwack" and felt the bolt's impact on his shield. He grunted and threw the shield which went sliding across the floor. Duke jumped up and raced toward the lance display. He ignored the sign that warned visitors not to touch the display. Grabbing the nearest lance, he prepared to defend himself. The attacker hurled the empty crossbow at Duke. He side-stepped. The crossbow crashed into the wall. The attacker ran.

Duke began to pursue his assailant but did not notice that several crossbow bolts were laying on the floor. Stepping on a bolt, he lost his footing and plunged to the floor. "This just isn't my day," he muttered. Quickly regaining his feet, he rushed out the door. Looking down the corridor, he saw the assailant had almost reached the intersection of the two halls. He followed as fast as he could, still carrying the lance. The assailant flew past the intersection and to the end of the north wing. There he entered a door to the left and disappeared from Duke's view. When Duke arrived at the end of the hall, he entered the same door and found a stairwell. He could hear the person's feet pounding up the steps near the top. A door opened and slammed. Duke pursued, now breathing hard. Perspiration was dripping down his forehead.

When Duke reached the top of the stairs, he flung open the door to be confronted by Adolph Hitler. He then remembered that the exhibits above the north wing featured photographs of people and events of the Second World War. The second floor was one large open room interspersed with support beams and filled with numerous displays. The displays were large and blocked his view. He saw no one and wondered if his attacker had found another exit. A loud creaking sound assured Duke that he was not alone in the room. Running toward the sound, he came into sight of his attacker straining to open a huge window. Apparently the window had not been used in many years and was painted shut. The person looked once at Duke and the lance he was carrying. The person backed up several feet, then charged the window.

Duke could hardly believe what happened next. The assailant crashed through the window and fell to the ground about 15 feet below. Splinters of wood and glass fell in a wide area. The assailant tumbled, got up, and ran down the adjoining street. Duke was dumbfounded. After staring a few seconds, he hurled the lance from the window in a futile gesture.

Duke had previously agreed to meet Linda for lunch. People gave him a few stares as he walked into the restaurant in his torn and battered clothing. Linda was seated at a table in the center of the main dining area. When she saw him enter the room, she hurriedly left her chair and came to him.

"What happened to you?" She asked with obvious concern. He

related his earlier plans for a peaceful museum visit and the wild confrontation he had experienced instead. As he finished his story, Linda kissed him with relief.

"Duke, I am so glad that you're not badly unhurt. Do you think you should see a doctor just to make sure?"

"I'm O.K." Duke reassured her.

"You must have been a sight trying to explain what happened to the museum attendant and the local police!"

"I don't think that I just happened to run into a nutcase," Duke said with a frown. "Maybe I'm paranoid, but that guy seemed to be there with the solitary purpose of killing me!"

"Duke, surely not." Linda reached out and touched his shoulder.

"Ouch," Duke responded. "My shoulder is a little sore." He added, "I think we both better be careful until this whole affair is sorted out."

"That's a good idea," Linda agreed. "We should keep up our guard while we finish our business tomorrow. We have to scope out the city and visit the two nearby possible sites of the proposed bottling plant."

After lunch, Linda had to return to work. She didn't leave Duke until he had given her numerous reassurances that he was okay. He said that he would survive with his bumps and bruises. He just wanted to return to the hotel and take it easy.

That evening Linda spent most of her time sorting through notes involving the installation of the super computer. Duke noticed that she had Coca-Cola's manual open to the section on security over automatic systems. She made great use of her laptop's CD-ROM drive. One CD was used to store over 175 separate reference guides, marketing information, and software applications. What once filled several bookshelves was now contained on a compact disk weighing less than an ounce. She could do research from almost any location now.

Duke wasn't feeling very sociable due to his injuries. He took some aspirin and retired to his room for the evening. Linda continued working late into the night. She used the modem in her laptop computer to connect via phone line to her desktop computer back home in Atlanta.

Chapter 14

The level of trade always corresponds to the state of diplomatic relations.

John Murphy, representative of the American-Soviet Trade and Economic Council (ASTEC)

"If we didn't need to check out the proposed sites for the bottling plant, I'd take you to the best spot for viewing Warsaw. Do you know where that is?" Linda quizzed Duke.

Without waiting for a response, Linda pointed to a tall building. "The best vantage point from which to admire Warsaw is from atop the 37-story Palace of Culture and Science. It's a wedding-cake skyscraper, given to the city by Stalin in 1955. That's the only spot in the city from which you can avoid looking at the ugly Stalin-Gothic style building."

"I like it," Duke said. "The Wedding Cake building."

"You would," Linda Lou laughed. "The landmark houses museums, theaters, libraries, swimming pools, restaurants, and the Academy of Science. It's the cultural center of Warsaw. Too bad we didn't get to hear a Chopin recital. Chopin was born just outside Warsaw."

Duke negotiated the blue Ford south. He pointed out the fine stucco facades of the 19th century houses. "They are not hidden by commercial signs yet," Linda grinned. After leaving Warsaw, Duke took E82, through Tomaszow Maz and Piotrkow Tryb, toward Czestochowa. The difficulties of the previous day were largely forgotten.

Duke asked, "I've seen a lot of flower peddlers in Warsaw. What's the holiday?"

"No holiday," Linda Lou replied, "There's an age-old Polish tradition of giving flowers on almost any occasion. There are many wealthy farmers who grow roses in glass-covered hothouses."

Horses pulled people in rickety wooden carts along the shoulder of the two-lane road. Farmers pitched hay onto wagons in the fields.

There were small fields of barley, wheat, cabbage, and potatoes. Duke noticed the small, box-shaped farmhouses on both sides of the road. Even the huts, however, had a T.V. antenna on top to watch the two state-owned channels. There are more than ten million television sets in Poland--one for every four people. There are VCRs, also. Every few miles they saw a cross or a shrine with a figure of the Madonna or Christ, with fresh-cut flowers.

Duke was driving behind a Polish-built Polonez auto as they entered the small town of Czestochowa, the home of the most revered religious shrine in Poland. Linda spoke, "I'm supposed to meet someone at the Dom Pielgrzyma, which is adjacent to the Jasna Gora complex." She checked her watch. "We're a little early, so let's go to the coffee shop."

The service was slow, so Linda pulled out an old brochure and started telling Duke about Poland's famous place of pilgrimage.

"The quest of so many walking pilgrims is Our Lady of Czestochowa, better known as the Black Madonna--not the rock singer in the states. Legend attributes the icon to St. Luke the Evangelist. By the way, Jasna Gora means Hill of Light."

Linda pointed to the photo in the brochure. "The painting shows the Madonna holding the Christ child in her left arm. The child is holding a book, known as a *Hogegetria.* The Poles credit the painting for saving their country in 1655. 'Our Lady' gave 230 defenders the strength to repel 4,000 Protestant Swedish invaders. The Jasna Gora basilica is Poland's only unconquered fortification."

"What are the two long marks on her right cheek?" Duke asked.

"Legend states that the scars on her face were inflicted by a would-be Tartar thief who found the icon getting heavier and heavier as he was stealing it. He apparently fell dead before he could complete the theft."

Pointing to the photo, Duke inquired again, "Why are their faces dark?"

"The original painting may have been from the Fifth century. Some scholars believe it is an exact image of the Virgin Mary; she was a young Jewish woman from Palestine and people from that region were dark complexioned."

"Bear in mind," Linda continued, "that the four foot by three foot icon was completely repainted in 1434 on three repaired cyprus planks allegedly from the top of the table of the Holy Family in Nazareth. A woven canvas was glued to the boards and the artists copied the original damaged painting."

Duke read the short description of the painting by the historian Canon Jan Dlugosz of Krakow:

"A picture of Mary, the most glorious and the most venerable virgin, the queen of the world and of the Poles, has a serene expression on Her face from whatever direction you look at it. Looking at this picture, one is pervaded with a sense of peculiar piety, as if looking at a living person."

"Nicholas! We are over here." Linda stood up and motioned to a thin, dark-headed person entering the door. When the man reached the table, Linda shook his hand and said, "Nicholas Ziegenbein, I want you to meet John Wayne Jones. We call him Duke. Have a seat." Nicholas was wearing a Coca-Cola uniform, with an open-neck shirt.

"I can't stay long. I still have some more deliveries to make," Nicholas replied in heavily accented English.

Linda spoke to Duke. "Nicholas is one of the few Protestants living in Poland. His great-grandfather was one of the 4,000 Swedish invaders who were repelled by the Poles at Jasna Gora basilica."

"Come on, Linda; don't make up stories. You'll get me in trouble," Nicholas responded cautiously.

"Don't worry about Duke. He tried to climb over the Wall into East Berlin. How's your son? He's about 13 now, right?"

"He's 12. My whole family is doing fine." Nicholas appeared nervous to Duke.

Looking at Duke, Linda said, "Nicholas drives a Coke truck in this area. He also repairs machinery on the side." Turning back to Nicholas she asked, "Do you still have to sign a list every morning for two months in order to buy a washing machine in Poland?"

Nicholas broke his first smile and said, "Yeah, a businessman has many headaches in Poland. I have arranged for you to take a tour of Jasna Gora with a priest who spent some time in the U.S.A. He's going to guide some American tourists at 1:15. Let us walk over and meet him." Nicholas rose.

Duke took a last sip from his cup of tea. On his way to the check-out counter, he overheard Linda ask Nicholas, "Have there been any problems with any of the Coke machines?"

"No, they're working perfectly," was Nicholas' response.

At the monastery, Linda and Duke joined a tour group of Americans, most of them students and professors from Texas. They met Father Philip Nachowitz, who was to be their guide. As they walked through the courtyard, Duke noticed that the coat-of-arms of the Paulite Order was cleverly designed into the cobblestone.

After walking through the Lubomirski Gate, Father Nachowitz, who spoke excellent English, led the group into the Chapel of Our Lady, through a front door. He took the group of eighteen into the front of the Chapel while a service was proceeding. The Chapel was filled with worshipers singing "Ave Marie." As Duke entered, he noticed the Baroque stucco decorations in the main part of the interior of the church. There were four side altars and three portals of black marble. The vaulted ceilings were adorned with stucco patterns.

The ebony High Altar contained the Miraculous Picture, surrounded by silver angel ornaments. Above the altar was a pitched canopy of cloth. Duke tried to tiptoe on the black-and-white-marble floor as he moved to get a closer look at the Black Madonna. No photos were allowed.

Duke was able to see the coloration of the Madonna's face with the two scars. The Madonna and Child wore a gown, which was an elaborate overlay of gem-encrusted gold and silver. Before they had entered, Father Nachowitz indicated that the golden crowns over the heads of the Madonna and child were presented by Pope Pius X in 1910 in connection with the coronation of the icon.

After leaving the Chapel, the priest took the group to a large room containing many gifts received by the Paulite Order. He merely took a key pinned to his robe and unlocked the wooden door to the room. Duke noticed a simple alarm system attached to the door. There were thousands and thousands of gold and silver items, diamonds, rubies, and other precious stones in the glass-encased storage areas. Many wedding and diamond rings, brooches, old coins, tie tacs, and other ornaments were displayed in the large room.

Next, Father Nachowitz took the group to another room where most members bought some souvenirs. Linda bought a Coke from a bright red Coca-Cola machine, and seemed quite pleased. Outside, many of the tour members gave the priest a tip, which he gladly accepted. One professor got him to pose giving the Texas A&M Aggie sign, a fist with an uplifted thumb. What a sight in Poland, a Polish priest posing with a "gig-em" symbol. Shades of Solidarity.

Once Linda and Duke started driving toward Oswiecim, Duke began flipping through the book she had bought: *Shrine of the Black Madonna*, by Janusz St. Pasierb.

Almost talking to himself, Duke said, "This place has a collection of armor and firearms, musical instruments, portraits, old books, and records--Wow! Listen to this. There's a huge gold monstrance. What's a monstrance?"

"That's a vessel in which the consecrated Host is exposed for the veneration of the faithful," Linda spoke matter-of-factly.

"Anyway, there's two cloisonne high priests, Melchizedek and Aaron, holding their hands pointing to the Host. The crown has a large diamond, plus 2,366 diamonds, 2,208 rubies, 214 pearls, 81 emeralds, and 30 sapphires." Duke rubbed his finger tips over the glossy picture of the crown in the book.

He read for a time while Linda drove in silence. Finally he asked, "Did you know that there are five different robes for the Black Madonna? A ruby robe, a diamond robe--." Duke paused.

"What are the other three robes?" Linda asked quietly.

"I don't know. Can't find it in this book." Duke closed the book with a bang. "I hate books that leave you hanging!"

* * *

Their next stop was the Auschwitz concentration camp near

Oswiecim. The words on the gate are: Work Brings Freedom. Yet the only way out during four-and-one-half years was "through the chimney." The camp has been left as it was found by the Russians on January 27, 1945 as a grim reminder. From the watch tower at the entrance, they saw the enormity of the largest Nazi death camp. The barracks and crematoria are now museums of the Nazi atrocities, where over four million people from 29 nationalities were brought to die after being told they were moving to resettlement areas.

As the people debarked from their train, an S.S. physician determined the fate of the prisoners with either of two words--right or left. About 75 percent of the people were directed straight into the gas chambers--after they removed their clothes. The exhibits showed how progressively efficient the Nazis became. Shooting was too slow, so they built a gas chamber. Duke shivered as he imagined an S.S. efficiency expert moving through the camp making observations and calculations.

There was a huge bin of 5,000 children's shoes, a large bin of false legs, a bin of hair--all being saved by the Nazis. After the gas chamber, gold was removed from corpses' teeth. The horrible sights such as photos of lamps made of skin gave Duke creepy feelings. One exhibit indicated that twins were especially important for the human experiments performed by the S.S. doctors at the camp.

Later outside Linda asked Duke, "Well, can Coke locate the plant site here?"

Duke breathed slowly and responded, "Ask me tomorrow."

Thinking about the Nazis and World War II, Duke remembered the graphic D-Day battle depicted in the hit movie, Saving Private Ryan. Prior to the movie, Duke had watched a D-Day television special hosted by retired General H. Norman Schwrzkopf. The Desert Storm hero walked among the huge allied cemetery on the French coastline near the famous invasion site. Thousands of crosses provided a final testimony to the faith of soldiers who made the ultimate sacrifice on the Normandy beaches. Scattered here and there among the crosses were Star of David grave markers for the Jewish soldiers who perished along side their Christian comrades. Military casualties were enormous in World War Two's European theater for both sides.

One of the most incredible events of the D-Day battle was where Colonel James Earl Rudder led his battalion of army rangers against a German gun fortress atop the 100-foot Cliffs of Pointe de Hoc. From this strategic position, overlooking the Normandy beaches, the German guns could wreak havoc among the allied invasion forces. Rudder's rangers gallantly attacked the German positions. Nazi soldiers fired machine guns and tossed grenades straight down at the American soldiers, but in the end the American fighting spirit prevailed against seemingly impossible odds. Following his distinguished military career, Rudder served as president of Texas A&M University from 1959 to 1970.

After a short drive to Krakow, the ancient seat of the Polish Kings, the couple stopped at Orbis-Holiday Inn for the night. Linda checked in with her supervisors and discovered that Duke was needed back in Atlanta. Moses requested that Duke return on the next available flight. Duke was dismayed by the news, but complied and booked a flight leaving in the morning.

The next day Linda and Duke drove back toward Warsaw on E7, passing through Kielce and Radom, to Okecie Airport, about six miles south of Warsaw. Linda planned to travel to Moscow for a few days. They kissed goodbye at the airport. Duke caught a Lot flight at 6:35 to Frankfurt, connecting with an American Airlines 747 direct flight to Atlanta.

Chapter 15

"Coke is it!"

Once the alarm system was compromised, the thin figure took off a ski mask, gloves, and a heavy coat. He put the gloves back on as he walked toward a Coca-Cola machine. Only after drinking a Classic Coke and eating some peanut butter crackers did the silent figure go to work.

Taking a crowbar, the dark intruder broke into a treasure room and moved to the nearest glass-enclosed case. He placed a larger flashlight face down on the glass and turned it on. Next, a large suction cup was placed on top of the glass, and a round circle was cut with a glass cutter. After moving the round piece of glass to the floor, his gloved hands retrieved the jewelry and other precious items and placed them into one of several brown cloth sacks. Methodically, the prowler emptied nineteen other glass-enclosed cases. When a sack was full, he took the full sack and placed it into the secret compartment from where he started.

After the remaining eleven storage cases were emptied, the thief broke into another storage room. The diamonds on the Diamond Robe sparkled as the light of his flashlight hit them. The jeweled robe disappeared into a cloth sack. Two other gem-encrusted gowns were placed on top of the Diamond Robe. Looking like the Grinch who stole Christmas, the robber placed the heavy sack over his shoulder and carried it back to a second secret compartment. This second hiding place was almost full, so the thin prowler became more selective on his return to the storage room.

He decided against taking the reliquary of St. Paul the Hermit -- no gems on it. But his small hands gently placed the reliquary of the Holy Cross into his cloth sack. He liked the very large blue stone on it. He softly counted the number of precious stones on a crosier showing the Holy Trinity. There were 22 rubies and two large sapphires. The last item placed into his sack was a monstrance with a golden crown on top. After dragging the sack back to the secret compartment, he found that the sack would not fit. He pulled out the monstrance, closed the door, and wrapped the monstrance in another sack. He placed the sack next to the Coca-Cola machine, and began drinking another Coke.

He had not found the Ruby gown. "It must be on the Black Madonna," he thought. He walked to the storage area, and put a rosary and a golden chain into his pockets. Then he walked into the library, and shined his flashlight onto the white polychrome ceiling painting. He rested in a large armchair with the coat-of-arms of the Paulite Order. "Not very comfortable," he said softly.

Retracing his steps, he began picking up his equipment -- suction cup, glass cutter, ski mask, and the heavy coat. "Wait a minute." He put everything down, and walked over and retrieved the two Coke crates. After placing them next to the drink machine, he put on his coat, and stuffed the ski mask into his right coat pocket. He picked up the sack with the monstrance, walked over to the window next to the door, and cut a round hole in it. He then opened the window, climbed out, shut the window, and placed the round piece of glass on the ground. Cautiously he made his way through the Lubomirski Gate, across the courtyard, and disappeared into the still morning darkness. In forty more minutes the sun would shine on the Shrine of the Black Madonna.

* * *

Not until the second day after the burglary did it become public. A spokesperson for the Polish Catholic church indicated that there had been a significant robbery at the Jasna Gora Monastery. A reward of two million zoltys was offered for the recovery of the stolen sacred artifacts. The spokesperson assured the world that the priceless Black Madonna was safe.

An official of the Polish government stated that the robbery probably had been planned by a few radical Solidarity members to further sabotage General Jaruzelski's successful program to improve Poland's economic situation. A socialist organization maintained that the "irresponsible hand of the CIA" was involved in the "breaching of the security system" at the holy shrine. The U.S. State Department denied any knowledge of the unfortunate theft and offered any aid available in recovering the stolen religious treasures.

A spokesman for Lech Walesa, a Solidarity leader, said that the desperadoes would be found and punished. Many of the underground newspapers began carrying the following account of the robbery. "The bandits might have had inside help because the alarm system was off during the entry into the monastery. The only other logical conclusion is that someone forgot to switch on the silent alarm system -- a highly coincidental accident. Or else the alarm system was faulty, which an official of the Paulite Order denied."

Another underground newspaper indicated that the Diamond Robe, two other gowns, and the priceless "Aaron and Melchizedek" monstrance were part of the stolen artifacts. The robbers apparently made no attempt to take the Black Madonna, who fortunately was wearing the Ruby Robe.

Chapter 16

Goods are usually produced in a factory -- and then sold. By contrast, services are often sold first, then produced.

Jerome McCarthy and William Perreault, Jr.

Moses was deeply troubled by the threats to Duke's life and by some very disturbing findings from his investigations. Consequently, Moses had asked Duke to return home early from his European trip with Linda. In less than an hour, Moses had to leave for the airport to pick him up. Moses was not looking forward to the homecoming. Duke would be disconcerted with what Moses had uncovered.

At least Moses had some good news concerning the impact of his expert witness testimony. The trial judge had issued his decision in the Coke vs. Tropicana lawsuit. The court found that the Tropicana Premium Pack orange juice television commercial was misleading because of its false visual portrayal of its orange juice. The visual sequence of Mr. Jenner squeezing juice from the orange and pouring it directly into cartons was false. Tropicana orange juice is not squeezed from the orange directly into cartons, since Tropicana orange juice is pasteurized first and sometimes even frozen. Mr. Jenner's qualifying statement in the commercial--it's pure pasteurized juice as it comes from the orange -- is unacceptable because pasteurized juice does not come directly from oranges.

According to the issued opinion, the ad communication test showed a level of consumer confusion above 15%. In the court's opinion, that was a substantial number of consumers to be misled. Thus, there was sufficient evidence of risk of irreparable harm. Thus, Coca-Cola was granted an injunction against the Tropicana Premium Pack orange juice television commercial. Moses felt that his expert testimony had been helpful to his employer, Coca-Cola.

* * *

Meanwhile, Linda was attending an international seminar

concerning ethics. It wasn't something she had chosen, but the higher-ups at Coca-Cola thought it worthy of attention. The two day seminar was being held in Moscow. Linda had been slightly shocked when she arrived at the best hotel in Moscow, the Mezhdunarodnaja. The modern hotel looked like a Hyatt Regency, with a large open inside area with five glass elevators serving thirteen floors. Inside the lobby was a bright red Coke machine--Ko-Ka Kora. However, about 20 minutes were required to purchase a token for one dollar to obtain the Coke. The machine was serviced by a German firm.

Inside the lobby, there was a tubular American Express money machine with several advertisements displayed on it. The shops in the hotel took only hard currency and not rubles. Linda walked on the white tile floor to look at one of the many birch trees inside the lobby. The trunk of the tree was real, but the branches and leaves were fake. There were bright maroon carpets, chairs, and round tables around a water fountain with several large pools containing large red fish. There was a large, wooden clock seven stories high with a rooster on top. While she was checking into the hotel, the rooster began to crow on the hour, flapping its wings, and two wooden men began blowing their horns. What a sight.

Things really had changed in Moscow due to Mikhail Gorbachev's glasnost. Linda thought about a conversation she had with Moses just before her trip. Moses told her of the amazing new openness at former Soviet universities. The university in Tbilisi had invited a group of American professors to lecture audiences of students and professors about the relevance of Christianity to the academic world. After decades of government-enforced atheism, the professors were surprisingly more open-minded on spiritual issues than many of their American counterparts. One of the American lecturers, Dr. William Jordan, Associate Professor of Mechanical Engineering at Louisiana Tech University, traced the origins of science and discussed the Christian faith of many of the early scientists, such as Galileo. Dr. Jordan emphasized that he believed there was no substantial conflict between faith and science. Dr. Jordan was the first person to talk about God at that university in over 70 years.

Dr. Jordan's perspective was reinforced by two books, *The Fingerprint of God* and *Creation and Time*. The author of both books, an astrophysicist, Dr. Hugh Ross, described a growing movement among cosmologists in which the universe was regarded to be a result of intelligent design. The books extensively referenced past and current scientific research regarding the origin of the universe. Ross concluded that the universe is at least ten billion orders of magnitude ($10^{10,000,000,000}$ times) too small and too young for life to have assembled itself by natural processes.

Linda was surprised to see people openly carrying Bibles around with them. She remembered when the new import rules became effective and allowed Bibles to be brought into Russia and the surrounding countries. Several groups in the United States began sending free Bibles. Muscovites lined up in hundreds to get a copy. The *Wall Street Journal* reported that over a million Bibles were sent in one year, but even that number was far short of the demand.

The seminar on ethics was led by several renowned businessmen representing different countries. At the opening breakfast, the director of the seminar set the mood for the day with the following statements: "When evaluating one's goals and objectives, a vital question must be asked. What is one's highest aspiration? The answer could be selected from the following: wealth, fame, knowledge, popularity, or integrity. Integrity is defined as the quality of being of sound moral principle, upright, honest, and sincere. If integrity is secondary to any of the alternatives, then it is subject to sacrifice in situations where a choice must be made. Such situations will inevitably occur in every person's life."

This caught Linda's attention.

The most intriguing session for Linda was one led by an American businessman. He made a connection between ethics and the size of the federal government.

"One of the problems facing some nations today is the burgeoning size of their federal government. What is the force that keeps the government expanding? Although the answer is complex and involves many issues, one driving force behind the growth of government is the decline of societal ethical values. Chuck Colson, a leading spokesman on ethics issues, stated that government is where 'people most often turn when lack of character becomes rampant in society; it is to the state that they turn for the benefits communities no longer provide.' If the business professions are unable to regulate themselves according to high ethical values, then the general public will inevitably demand that government provide more regulation. With more regulations comes more government bureaucracy."

"The growth of government expenditures above the amount of taxes collected results in large annual budget deficits and culminates in an enormous national debt. Besides its cost, another problem with a huge government is the manner it usurps individual freedoms." This last statement was met with a scattering of applause. The citizens of former communist countries could well understand the issue of too-large and too-intrusive national governments.

The American businessman continued, "My home country, America, was founded by persons who believed that only the highest moral and ethical character would ensure the nation's prosperity. James Madison, the fourth U.S. President, known as the father of the U.S. Constitution, made the following statements. I quote. 'We have staked the whole future of the American civilization not upon the power of government, far from it. We have staked the future ... upon the capacity of each and all of us to govern ourselves, to control ourselves, to sustain ourselves according to the Ten Commandments of God.'"

"I think there are certain, widely recognized values that are indicators of your ethical standing. Michael Josephson, a prominent Los Angeles ethicist, compiled a list he called the 'Ten Universal Values' which includes: honesty, integrity, promise-keeping, fidelity (loyalty), fairness, caring, respect for others, responsible citizenship, pursuit of excellence, and accountability. We need to ensure that these universal values are venerated in our business firms and in the countries where we live. Whether your roots are in the U.S., Latin America, Europe, Africa, or Asia; whether you are religious or nonreligious; we can all agree that these are values which ensure a free and orderly world."

Linda thought about her friends who were from many different backgrounds. They had some very significant differences, but they also shared some common values such as love of family, respect for truth, and respect for life. These values were essential for the welfare and progress of human society. She turned her attention back to the speaker.

"There is a basis for ethics or absolute standards, whether you derive it from natural law, Judeo-Christian revelation, or simply the accumulated wisdom of human civilization. Unfortunately, many people have rejected absolute standards and bought into the relativist approach. Using relative standards, an individual judges the correctness of an action depending on the person, situation, or results involved. Using relative standards, the Nazis justified everything they did, including the Jewish Holocaust. Adhering to absolute standards of ethics requires integrity and courage. It's much easier to 'go with the flow' than to speak out for what is right."

Linda had been so focused on the presentation that she was surprised when her stomach started grumbling. After looking at her watch, she deemed her stomach to be correct--it was time for lunch and she had skipped breakfast. The session ended before her stomach could cause her too much embarrassment.

The session after lunch was led by a female partner of one of the Big Five International accounting firms. She started out with a quote from *The CBS Murders*, by Richard Hammer.

"Margaret Barbera was very good with numbers. She could take a balance sheet, a set of account books, invoices, bills, and more, juggle and manipulate the figures and, presto, thousands became millions, losses became profits, profits became losses, sales soared or fell, whatever her employer desired, and it would take an expert auditor knowing precisely where to look and what to look for to figure out what she'd done, and even then, it still might slip by."

"There is an underground of people like Margaret Barbera, eagerly sought after by unethical businessmen in trouble, especially in volatile and unstable industries, such as garments and jewelry. Ask the right questions of the right people, and pretty soon a Margaret Barbera, or somebody very much like her, will come knocking at the door."

She continued. "Individual responsibility is the critical issue in establishing a code of conduct. A code of professional conduct is formulated to provide a minimum level of conduct for the well-being of a profession. The American Institute of CPAs' Code of Professional Conduct describes the responsibility of the CPA to colleagues, clients, and the general public."

"Either you follow the profession's code, or you get expelled from the AICPA. One reason we have a professional code of conduct is to provide some uniformity in the way different CPAs respond to similar situations. There are four distinct parts of the AICPA's Code: Principles of Professional Conduct, Rules of Conduct, Interpretations of Rules of Conduct, and Ethics Rulings. The principles of professional conduct address the following: accountant's responsibilities, serving the public interest, integrity, objectivity and independence, due care, and scope of services."

"The Rules of Conduct provide the minimum levels of acceptable conduct. They are enforced by the Ethics Division of the AICPA. The Interpretations and Ethics Rulings provide additional guidance."

After a question and answer period, the session ended.

Before retiring to bed that night, Linda sent Duke a quick e-mail. She also decided to write him just to test how long an air mail letter takes.

> Dear Great One,
>
> I'm looking out of the 12th floor, room 1241 in the best Moscow hotel. I can see a large river, smoke stacks, pollution, and one of the eight Stalin buildings. Most of the buildings are made of dull red bricks. There is very little traffic on the road at this time. My room is surprisingly large. Wall paper. TV. Two single beds. Bathroom works.
>
> All is fine. The conference has been very

informative. I saw Red Square and the Cathedral of St. Basil yesterday. Also went to Gum Department Store.

I miss you. It's not as much fun here without you. By the time you get this letter, I'll already be back in the States. If you didn't take me out to dinner upon my return, you're in trouble!

Love, Linda Lou

The next night, after the final session of the seminar, Linda went with a group to the famous round Bolshoi Theatre to see a Polish ballet. The stately and brightly decorated interior featured six rows of red velvet upholstery and gilded boxes with sparkling cutglass chandeliers. The frieze in front had red flags and two images of Lenin. Figures of many people appeared on the round ceiling. The ballet was a bizarre, avant-garde program with many symbols. There was little clapping from the audience, and a number of people left early. Linda wished she had just gone to bed early.

* * *

On the flight from Moscow, Linda came across an interesting ad in the airline magazine. The ad was titled "Fly a Mig-29 at Mach 2.5 in Moscow." A company named MIGS Etc. was offering high-performance military flight packages. The customer would be accompanied by a top Russian test pilot. Linda decided she would definitely plan to do this her next trip to Moscow. After crossing the Atlantic, her plane landed in New York. She changed planes for a connecting flight to Atlanta. On the final leg of her journey, she thought about how busy her life had become. She had been so involved with work that she had little time for anything else--until Duke had wandered into her life.

When the plane landed, she was glad that Duke would be there to greet her at the "Big Hustle" airport terminal. Funny. Atlanta's biggest employer is the airport. This business trip had been far more interesting than most. She really wished Duke had not been called back early by that Professor McDonald. Duke would have made the return trip much more enjoyable.

Linda was adventuresome by nature. She considered herself very competent. She liked a good challenge, meeting new people, and going to new places. She was extremely independent. So where did Duke fit in? There was so much he didn't know about her. If she revealed all, how would he react? She was perplexed.

The plane taxied around the Hartsfield International Airport an insufferably long time after landing -- even for Atlanta. Finally, the passengers were told they could disembark. As usual, many people had already stood up to get their carry-on bags, before the plane came to a complete stop at the terminal.

As she walked from the plane, it was easy to spot Duke in the crowd. Duke's gray eyes met hers. They were cold. He wasn't smiling. "What's wrong," she thought. Now they were only a few feet away from each other. Suddenly she noticed two Atlanta cops standing beside Duke.

"That's her," he said sadly.

Her heart was in her throat. She could not take a breath. Her mind raced with thoughts. "They can't know. Duke, Duke, what have you done?" She felt the policeman's hands take her wrists. He handcuffed her. She did not resist. The other policeman told her what her rights were. It seemed like a dream--no, a waking nightmare. A shudder came over her. As they escorted her to the police car, she looked over at Duke. He would not look at her.

After driving her to the downtown police station, she was taken to an interrogation room. Duke came into the small room. The officers left and locked the door, leaving Duke and her alone.

"The evidence points to you," he said angrily. He sat down hard in one of the wooden, straight-back chairs. In a more subdued voice, he added, "I thought you were someone special."

"Duke, I love you." She choked on the words.

"That doesn't matter," Duke said painfully. "While we were in Poland, Moses cracked the case. He asked me to fly home early to prepare me for this wonderful reunion. He was afraid you might try to frame me and drag me down with you. I didn't believe him at first, but then he showed me the evidence of what you've been doing."

He looked sternly into Linda Lou's eyes. Linda shook her head. "That's not true," she said softly. Duke frowned at her comment. He continued. "You tried to kill me. You killed one of Moses' students."

Duke paused, then continued. "The night after we left on our trip, Moses used the electronic spying equipment that I originally purchased to tap the computer of Kirby Forrest. I thought Forrest was our Coke culprit. Moses thought Forrest was too obvious. Turns out Moses was right. He had a hunch that your computer knowledge would make it possible for you to pull off the Coke computer system shenanigans. But what really tipped him off was when he discovered that you had worked with Forrest before he retired from Coke. You probably learned his computer password at that time and used it to throw us off your trail. You clandestinely entered the Coke computer system using a Trojan Horse program. I can't determine whether you wrote the program or simply discovered it. No matter, we got rid of it."

"To make a long story short, Moses parked in front of your apartment and recorded images from your computer. Using a modem on each end, you used your laptop computer in Poland to dial into your desktop microcomputer back home in Atlanta. You then examined the inventory records, and the Diet Coke formula you had derived from those records. You even made the mistake of receiving messages of offers to buy the formula over your computer's modem from several individuals in India. Moses has it all on video tape."

"What! How?" Her face paled.

Duke ignored her question. "You decided to sell the Diet Coke formula to your contacts in India for four million dollars. Not bad pay for a marketer. However, four million doesn't seem to be enough to satisfy your greed. We also know you're connected with the theft of artifacts from the Jasna Gora religious site."

Linda tried to interrupt, but Duke continued.

"After the Poland theft made the papers a few days ago, Moses figured it might be related to those Coke machines. Moses remembered that sales were down dramatically after the old drink machines were replaced. The declining sales stuck out like a sore thumb on the monthly sales reports. Why would sales decline due to new machines? He called the Poles. They checked out the drink machines. Most of the religious artifacts were found in the two secret compartments in the backs of the machines. The police then apprehended Nicholas Ziegenbien at home. He had already taken a few items to his house, and there was no way he could deny the theft. He immediately confessed that you were the mastermind behind the operation. He said you arranged to have those specially reconstructed machines placed at the site four months ago. I overheard you ask him if he was having any problems with the machines."

"He's lying. Don't you have any faith in me, Duke?" Linda asked.

"You're not the person I thought you were." Duke slowly shook his head. "You're not going to make a fool out of me any longer! I haven't been able to break into all your computer files yet, but eventually I will. And when I do, I suspect I'll find a program that sends subliminal messages about flying."

"Duke, you must believe me," she pleaded. "I don't know anything about subliminal messages!"

Duke stood up slowly and said, "I can't believe a word you say."

Linda looked into Duke's eyes. When their eyes met, she thought his gaze would burn a hole through her. She was totally shattered.

With a shake of his head, Duke turned and walked quickly out of the room. He decided to go back to work on his dissertation. Being a graduate student was certainly safer than being a consultant for Coca-Cola. No one will try to kill you or break your heart.

* * *

The front page headline in the *Atlanta Constitution* on

Thursday proclaimed: "Black Madonna Trips Marketer's Scheme." A copyrighted story by Bill Batchelor began as follows:

> In Poland, the Black Madonna was almost ripped off by Nicholas Ziegenbien, an employee of Coca-Cola. He attempted to steal artifacts from the Jasna Gora, the religious site of the Black Madonna. He almost pulled it off with the help of two Coca-Cola machines with false-backs. Two alert consultants uncovered the scheme. Dr. Moses McDonald, at Georgia State University and Mr. John W. Jones---

Chapter 17

Honor is better than honors.
Abraham Lincoln

Duke was relaxing in the badly worn, broken recliner in the center of his apartment living room. The room was dimly lit by a single wall lamp standing in the corner farthest from the entrance. Although the antique mantle clock was about to chime five o'clock in the morning, he didn't feel much like sleeping. He had sat all night in that old chair. Ever since Linda's arrest five days ago, Duke had been in a dark mood. He despised thinking about her but he couldn't think about anything else. Moses had tried cheering Duke in every way imaginable, but the efforts had been futile. Just as Duke decided to take his gloom into the bedroom, perhaps to sleep an hour before the sun came up, the doorbell rang.

"What the devil," he muttered to himself. He walked reluctantly to the entrance door and peered through the peephole. Unsteadily, his hand turned the deadbolt. Duke opened the door to verify that he was seeing correctly.

"I apologize for the early hour, but I had too see you," his visitor said.

Rarely at a loss for words, Duke could only stare.

"Please, invite me in. Hear my strange tale and then decide if we can still be friends."

"Linda Lou, are you real or an apparition?" Duke paused for a moment, then frowned. "You've either made bail or escaped from jail," he said matter-of-factly.

Linda walked past Duke into the poorly lit living room. She sat on the sofa facing Duke's recliner and said softly, "I know I've hurt you, but I had no choice. Just listen, please."

Duke closed the door a little harder than necessary and crossed the room to face Linda. "I'm all ears," he said rather crossly, but deep in his heart he hoped that she had an explanation for her recent behavior.

"Sit, please," she gently requested.

Duke hadn't realized he was standing but he returned to his customary position in the recliner. He never took his eyes off Linda.

She reached into the inside pocket of her linen blazer and extracted its contents. She extended her hand toward Duke. She held a glistening metal badge. "Take it," she said.

Duke could reach her hand without rising from the recliner. He took her offering. As he scrutinized it, his left eyebrow arched. "Interpol? Isn't that some sort of international spy operation?"

"Actually, it's the International Criminal Police Organization. My area of expertise is industrial espionage between large international business firms, nonprofit organizations, or government entities. Interpol was asked to intervene in the Diet Coke formula case. I was the chief operative in the investigation. My cover was my job as Chuck Morgan's assistant; however, he never knew the true reason I was assigned to work for him."

"I really want to believe all this, Linda Lou, but you have to answer a few questions."

"If I can, I will." Her eyes showed her sincerity.

"First," he said. "Who actually stole the formula?"

"No one. Kirby Forrest was contacted by foreign agents, that is, the employees of an organization based in Bombay. Initially they were very civil and tried to buy the Diet Coke formula. Later, however, their civility transformed into hostility. They demanded that the formula be given to them. Kirby rejected the substantial bribes they offered. Ultimately, Kirby and members of his family were harassed and threatened. My job was to obtain the hard evidence needed to nail the villains."

Duke interrupted. "What about the inventory data you gathered using Kirby Forrest's computer password?"

Linda smiled. "Duke, you can't fool the bad guys without something to prove you're on the level. That data enabled me to deceive them, but surely you don't believe it could actually be used to derive the formula?"

"Well, actually, ..." Duke felt awkward.

Linda didn't wait for Duke to finish before continuing. "You and Professor McDonald created some real problems for me. First, you alarmed the foreign agents with your investigation. Next, and much worse, they decided to eliminate you by either threat, poison powder, crossbow bolt, or subliminal suggestion. I tried to protect you by staying close." Linda paused. "I suppose I got a little too close." She paused again and looked deeply into Duke's eyes. "I really fell for you, Duke. I've never before done anything like that. But then I've never before known anyone like you."

"Anyway," she resumed her monologue. "I arranged for you to go to Eastern Europe with me. That was supposed to slow down McDonald and you."

"Then, you knew beforehand about the theft at the Polish monastery," Duke interjected.

"No, actually Professor McDonald gets all the credit for that episode. As part of my Coke job I was merely checking to see that the Coke machines had been repaired. I was as astonished as anyone that Nicholas Ziegenbien accused me of masterminding the robbery. Believe me, I was genuinely upset when I was greeted at the airport by the Atlanta police and you. Thanks for helping me empathize with people who are arrested. Indeed, the experience was very insightful."

Duke felt remorse. "Linda Lou, I'm sorry. I didn't know."

"How could you?" She smiled. "Water under the bridge. Besides, I wasn't in jail for long before the police verified my credentials."

"I just wish you had told me all this earlier."

"Believe me, Duke, I wanted to tell you sooner. But I just couldn't. For one thing I couldn't jeopardize the operation. People's lives were in danger, including yours."

Linda and Duke continued talking for over an hour. At the end of their conversation, they simply stared at each other. After several minutes Duke slowly shook his head. "This is really unbelievable."

To which, Linda retorted, "Fact is stranger than fiction."

Duke stood and reached out to Linda. He pulled her up into his arms for a warm embrace. He softly said, "Linda Lou, I love you."

Chapter 18

Gateway to India

One of the world's largest cities, Bombay is a thriving, bustling seaport built on an island featuring India's finest harbor. In the congested streets of Bombay, people of diverse backgrounds mingle and coexist, usually peacefully.

The city is a mixture of old and new buildings, and in many ways resembles a big European city. In the area named Apollo Bunder, stands the "Gateway to India," an impressive arch built in 1907 to commemorate the visit of King George V and Queen Mary of England. Not far from that arch is an innocuous old cafe. At mealtimes, the establishment's main dining room is filled with savory odors of freshly prepared meals and the dinner talk of a hundred diners. Conversations were in various languages such as Marathi, Gujarati, and "Bombay Bat," a local dialect which includes words from several languages.

The bright lights of the main dining room were a stark contrast to the murky atmosphere of a small, secluded room located in the rear portion of the cafe. Two arched doorways on the same wall provided entrance to the room. Three tables with chairs stood in the center of the room. Two benches stood against the far wall opposite the doorways. On one bench, barely visible in the shadows, sat two men wearing turbans and long robes.

The only light in the room came from a small chandelier hanging directly above the center table. Seated at the table was a lone female dressed in a black evening gown. In front of her were two crystal decanters, each containing a dark liquid. Except for her barely noticeable breathing, she seemed a statue. Only her eyes moved when the two men dressed in Western-style dark, pin-striped business suits entered and sat next to the woman. In the next moment, three grim bodyguards followed. They remained standing, their knee-length coats almost concealed the weapons each carried. She looked into the face of the older businessman. He was seated on her right, the other businessman on her left.

"Viday, I thought you trusted me." Linda's face showed a hurt look.

The older man grinned disdainfully. "This is not a game," he hissed. "Where is your merchandise?"

"Relax," she said after a pause. She raised her right hand. The three bodyguards jerked slightly. She said again, "Relax," and snapped her fingers.

A waitress entered carrying a tray holding four glasses. She placed two in front of each businessman. The waitress left the room. Linda reached for the two glasses in front of Viday. She poured some liquid from the first decanter into a glass. She then took the other glass and poured some liquid from the second decanter. She pushed the glasses back to Viday. She then performed the same procedure for Viday's associate.

"Thirsty?" she asked.

Viday scowled. He sipped from the first glass and then, the second. His associate did likewise.

"The same," he mumbled. His accomplice nodded slightly.

"One is the bottled soft drink and the other is my formula," she said.

"How can I be certain?"

Linda reached into a sash at her waist and extracted a three and a half inch computer diskette. "My formula and supporting data are on the disk. You've already examined my preliminary work. You know it's valid. Now, where's my compensation?"

Viday's associate first looked at the older man for approval and then retrieved a leather pouch from his inner coat pocket. He pushed the pouch along the table to Linda. She examined its contents, which were stock certificates of several major international corporations. "Okay," she said as she casually tossed the disk to Viday.

He snagged the disk with both hands. "I don't care for your manner," he growled.

"The feeling is mutual." She gave him a dazzling smile. With a frown, the two businessmen rose from their chairs. When they did, a score of men rushed in through both entrances. They wore navy blue fatigues, helmets, and flak jackets. More noticeable than their apparel were the Israeli-built submachine guns in their hands. Almost as one, the three bodyguards drew identical foreign-made weapons.

"Stop," Viday yelled.

The three bodyguards dropped their weapons to the floor with a clatter.

"Bloodshed would be futile. This hand is lost but the game is not over." Viday looked menacingly toward Linda and said, "You have betrayed us."

"That's the bottom line, Sherlock," she quipped.

She turned toward the commando standing nearest her. "Perfect timing on your arrival, Hadji," she said.

"Thanks," Hadji responded. "Timing is everything in our business." He smiled and said, "I'm glad you're okay."

The leader of the commandoes faced Viday. "You are under arrest for industrial espionage and extortion. All of you will follow me." Viday, his associate, and the three bodyguards were led from the room. The commandoes followed, leaving Linda with the two men sitting in the shadows.

"At last, case closed." She released a long sigh. The two men behind her rose silently. The taller one walked toward Linda. She was looking toward a doorway and did not see his approach. His hands reached toward her and closed on her shoulders. A shudder ran through her.

"Linda Lou, thank God you're safe," he said in a barely audible voice.

She turned and grinned. "Most jobs aren't this exciting." He laughed; then he kissed her. After that, John Wayne Jones flatly stated, "Funny, all this espionage has worked up my appetite. Would you care for a bite to eat? I'm told this place has great food." He looked over his shoulder to where his companion stood. "How about it, Moses?"

"Two's company and three's a crowd, besides Katie's waiting for me at the Bombay Hilton. We can talk later." A feeling of deep camaraderie passed among the trio, then Professor Moses McDonald strode from the room. As he departed he thought, "I really should write down the details of this escapade. It would be fine reading for my students."

Epilogue

"Six-ton trucks and tricycle carts"

In late 1993, the Coca Cola Company returned to India after being away 16 years. The company formed a strategic alliance with Parle Exports, providing access to Parle's bottling network and a base for marketing Coke's international brands. To get the ball rolling, Coke's initial investment in India amounted to $60 million. Among other things, this money was used to renovate bottling plants. To reach the 896 million people of India, a fleet of six-ton delivery trucks was used to make direct-store deliveries. Additionally, small tricycle carts, fitted for pallet loading, were used to make deliveries to hard-to-reach customers located along narrow alleys.

* * * *

Following a one-year courtship, Duke Jones and Linda Lou Barfoot were married in Atlanta, Georgia. They took a honeymoon trip to Moscow where each flew in a Mig-29 fighter jet. They like to say that they started their married life at over twice the speed the sound.

APPENDICES

APPENDIX 1: TEST QUESTIONS

1. An indicator of market potential is:
   a. technological factors
   b. demographics
   c. political-legal environment
   d. all of the above

   (Ans. d, Ch. 1, p. pp. 8-9)

2. _____ decision making means that most decisions are made by one person or committee.
   a. obtuse
   b. decentralized
   c. centralized
   d. dynamic

   (Ans. c, Ch. 1, p. 15)

3. Types of audit reports do NOT include _____.
   a. qualified opinion
   b. adverse opinion
   c. denigrated opinion
   d. disclaimer

   (Ans. c, Ch. 2, p 17)

4. In an audit, an "unqualified opinion" means:
   a. the auditor did not have enough information to form an opinion.
   b. the financial statements are not presented fairly.
   c. the financial statements are fairly presented.
   d. the financial statements are not in accordance with GAAP.

   (Ans. c, Ch. 2, p. 17)

5. The _____ is to provide, in a timely and effective manner, all the financial information needed by managers, throughout the organization, so that they can make the best possible decisions.
   a. production information system (PIS)
   b. engineering information system (EIS)
   c. accounting information system (AIS)
   d. distribution information system (DIS)

   (Ans. c, Ch. 2, p. 18)

6. Operational audits are concerned with whether a firm is achieving _____ goals and objectives.
   a. financial
   b. nonfinancial
   c. both a and b
   d. none of the above

   (Ans. c, Ch. 2, p. 19)

7. In an interview, _____ generally indicates the person is telling the truth.
   a. avoiding eye contact
   b. quick answers and denials
   c. abnormal eye-blink rate
   d. restlessness

   (Ans. b, Ch. 2, p. 21)

8. A sample in which each population member has an equal probability of being selected is called a:
   a. simple random sample
   b. equality sample
   c. random generator
   d. none of the above

   (Ans. a, Ch. 2, p. 23)

9. What does a marketing information system NOT do:
   a. sorts information
   b. improvises information
   c. distributes information
   d. evaluates information

   (Ans. b, Ch. 2, p. 23)

10. Fraudulent techniques do NOT include _____.
   a. salami
   b. round-down
   c. pepperoni
   d. all the above
   e. both a and b, not c

   (Ans. e, Ch. 3, p. 26)

11. Marketing intermediaries help promote, sell, and distribute products to final buyers. These do NOT include _____.
   a. wholesalers and retailers
   b. warehouse and transportation firms
   c. government agencies
   d. ad agencies and media firms

   (Ans. c, Ch. 3, p. 27)

12. Coca-Cola cut short it's promotional campaign involving "Magicans" because it produced:
   a. a drop in sales
   b. negative publicity
   c. price wars
   d. distribution problems

   (Ans. b, Ch. 4, p. 35)

13. The budget provides information for each of the four elements of control. These do NOT include _____.
a. determining actions to perform
b. performing actions e.g. marketing research
c. assessing performance
d. comparison and follow-up

(Ans. b, Ch. 4, p. 37)

14. When Moses first met Duke, Moses _____.
a. was playing basketball
b. was startled by Duke’s motorcycle
c. was having a hot dog at the Varsity
d. prying open a Magican of Coca Cola

(Ans. b, Ch. 4, pp. 39-40)

15. When a company uses separate promotional campaigns for each of their market segments, it is called:
a. promotional mix
b. market positioning
c. decentralized marketing
d. differentiated marketing

(Ans. d, Ch. 5, p. 43)

16. Diet Coke's position within the market was based on its:
a. low calorie benefit
b. good taste
c. strong marketing
d. all of the above

(Ans. d, Ch. 5, p. 43)

17. What was on the back of Duke's motorcycle helmet?
a. picture of a ninja warrior
b. the words: "Auditors run on GAAS"
c. picture of a ballerina
d. the words: "Proud to be an American"

(Ans. a, Ch. 5, p. 44)

18. What's the unmentionable P-word?
a. Perestroika
b. Patagonia
c. Pepsi
d. preferred customer

(Ans. c, Ch. 5, p. 45)

19. Regarding disaster recovery planning, _____ businesses hit by a fire could not survive the 90 days necessary to rebuild a destroyed computer system.
a. 10 percent
b. 25 percent
c. 75 percent
d. 100 percent

(Ans. c, Ch. 5, p. 46)

20. _____ is an economic term that refers to the satisfaction you receive from consuming or using a product.
a. consumption
b. conspicuous consumption
c. demand
d. utility

(Ans. d, Ch. 5, p. 48)

APPENDIX 1: TEST QUESTIONS

21. _____ had dropped out of high school and worked as a farmer, oil drilling roughneck, logger, tire factory worker, G.I., and a college professor.

a. Linda Lou c. Duke's pop
b. Moses d. President Clinton

(Ans. c. Ch. 5, p. 50)

22. An objective of a sales promotion is to:

a. encourage brand switching
b. increase sales
c. motivate dealers to push the products
d. all of the above

(Ans. d, Ch. 5, p. 51)

23. _____ can wipe out programming, often can't be detected, and new ones are very difficult to detect.

a. Trojan Horse programs c. ZAP programs
b. Computer viruses d. Hackers

(Ans. b, Ch. 6, p. 58)

24. The average computer crime has been estimated to cost about _____.

a. $10,000 c. $100,000
b. $50,000 d. $600,000

(Ans. d, Ch. 6, p. 64)

25. Internal factors that should be considered when setting the price of a product include _____.
a. marketing objectives
b. market structure
c. government regulations
d. all the above

(Ans. a, Ch. 6, p. 65)

26. External factors that should be considered when setting the price of a product include _____.
a. marketing mix
b. market structure
c. marketing objectives
d. all the above

(Ans. b, Ch. 6, p. 65

27. The law of demand indicates that the quantity demanded of a good or service is _____ function of its price, *ceteris paribus*.
a. direct
b. inverse
c. converse
d. parallel

(Ans. b, Ch. 6, p. 66)

28. Ceteris paribus means _____.
a. prices are subject to change
b. holding everything else constant
c. beware the Ides of March
d. buyer beware

(Ans. b, Ch. 6, p. 66)

29. Changes (or shifts) of the demand curve do NOT result from changes in _____.
a. consumer preferences
b. consumer income
c. price of the product
d. prices of other products

(Ans. c., Ch. 6, p. 66)

30. Changes along the supply curve represent "changes in quantity supplied" caused solely by changes in _____.
a. level of technology
b. price of the product
c. costs of production
d. consumer preferences

(Ans. b, Ch. 6, p. 66)

31. The factors of production are defined as the inputs of _____.
a. land
b. capital
c. entrepreneurship
d. labor
e. all the above

(Ans. e., Ch. 6, p. 67)

32. A relatively _____ demand curve means that a product will sell close to the same quantity regardless of changes in price.
a. elastic
b. flexible
c. denigrated
d. inelastic

(Ans. d., Ch. 6, p. 68)

33. Schroeder and Moses consider _____ to be the greatest musician of all time.
a. Elvis c. Beethoven
b. Sinatra d. Ike Turner

(Ans. c, Ch. 7 p. 73)

34. First generation computers are characterized by _____.
a. large-scale integration c. integrated circuitry
b. vacuum tubes d. all the above

(Ans. b, Ch. 7 p. 77)

35. The big virus incident of 1988 that shut down 6,000 computers in the Internet loop was started by _____.
a. a college student c. Russian saboteurs
b. kindergarten students d. an industrial spy

(Ans. a, Ch. 7, p. 82)

36. _____ is defined as an independent appraisal function established within an organization to examine and evaluate the adequacy and effectiveness of the organization's internal control system and its overall quality of performance.
a. Internal auditing c. External auditing
b. Marketing analysis d. Perpetual review

(Ans. a, Ch. 7, p. 85)

37. Internal auditors specialize in areas such as _____ auditing
a. quality assurance
b. fraud
c. information systems
d. environmental
e. all the above

(Ans. e, Ch. 7, p. 86)

38. _____ describes the phenomenon of a consumer improperly reproducing the informational content of an advertisement.
a. ad insanity
b. information overload
c. distorted decoding
d. none of the above

(Ans. c, Ch. 8, p. 93)

39. The _____ shows the total assets, total liabilities, and total equity (net worth) of a business at a specific point in time.
a. income statement
b. balance sheet
c. statement of cash flows
d. budget

(Ans. b, Ch. 10, p. 110)

40. The _____ is widely used by financial analysts in assessing the investment potential of different stocks. This financial ratio is calculated by dividing the market price of the stock by the earnings per share.
a. current
b. P/E
c. return on equity
d. return on investment

(Ans. b, Ch. 10, p. 111)

APPENDIX 1: TEST QUESTIONS

41. Worldwide acceptance of international accounting standards will ultimately be determined by the _____.
a. IOSCO
b. AICPA
c. FASB
d. IASC

(Ans. a, Ch. 10, p. 111)

42. Marketing strategies do NOT include _____.
a. market penetration
b. diversification
c. product development
d. alienation

(Ans. d, Ch. 10, p. 112)

43. A growth strategy which concentrates on identifying new markets for existing products is called:
a. market penetration
b. diversification
c. market development
d. product development

(Ans. c, Ch. 10, p. 112)

44. _____ is where the buyer is unhappy with his or her purchase decision, and wonders whether the right choice was made.
a. Buyer's dilemma
b. Consumer confusion
c. Marketer's quotient
d. Cognitive dissonance

(Ans. d, Ch. 10, p. 112)

45. The buying process starts with:
a. problem recognition
b. information search
c. envy dissonance
d. none of the above

(Ans. a, Ch. 10, p. 113)

46. A typical new product has a life cycle made up of four stages that occur in this order: growth, introduction, decline, and maturity.
a. True b. False

(Ans. b, Ch. 10, p. 118)

47. The _____ shows the total assets, total liabilities, and total equity (net worth) of a business at a specific point in time.
a. income statement
b. balance sheet
c. statement of cash flows
d. budget

(Ans. b, Ch. 10, p. 110)

48. The set of people who take title, or assist in transferring title to a product as it goes from producer to consumer is called:
a. the product life cycle
b. the distribution channel
c. the product mix
d. commercialization

(Ans. b, Ch. 10, p. 118)

49. CRT is a marketing acronym for "consumer response tension."
a. True b. False

(Ans. b, Ch. 11, p. 123)

APPENDIX 1: TEST QUESTIONS

50. The Mall in Washington, D.C. is a _____.
    a. large indoor shopping mall with over 500 stores
    b. large outdoor shopping bazaar with over 1,000 booths
    c. broad expanse of land around which national monuments are situated
    d. lobby in the Capitol

    (Ans. c, Ch. 12, p. 128)

51. What problem would a businessman encounter in Russia:
    a. inadequate communication systems
    b. unreliable sources of supply
    c. relative worthlessness of the ruble
    d. all of the above

    (Ans. d, Ch. 12, pp. 134-135)

52. Variable cost varies directly with:
    a. fixed cost
    b. sales
    c. output
    d. all of the above

    (Ans. c, Ch. 13, p. 144)

53. While in Poland, Duke almost gets killed in a _____.
    a. car wreck
    b. museum
    c. plane crash
    d. boating accident

    (Ans. b, Ch 13, pp. 156-57)

APPENDIX 1: TEST QUESTIONS

54. During World War Two, army rangers attacked a German gun fortress atop the 100-foot cliffs of Pointe de Hoc in the battle of _____.

    a. the Bulge c. D-Day
    b. Bannockburn d. Vicksburg

    (Ans. c, Ch. 14, p. 167)

55. Using _____ standards, an individual judges the correctness of an action depending on the person, situation, or results involved. Using this approach to ethics, the Nazis justified everything they did, including the Jewish Holocaust.

    a. relative c. absolute
    b. declarative d. compounded

    (Ans. a, Ch. 16, p. 175)

56. Abraham Lincoln said, " _____ is better than honors."

    a. Victory c. Happiness
    b. Honor d. Peace

    (Ans. b., Ch. 17, p. 182)

END OF QUESTIONS

APPENDIX 2: TEAM PROJECT

The primary goal of the novel is to generate student enthusiasm and interest in the course material. Typically, an instructor will assign portions of the novel to be read throughout the term. Questions from selected portions of the novel would then be included on exams.

A second and more innovative application of the novel is as follows. The instructor can require students to work in teams and prepare a role-playing presentation based on some aspect of the novel. This assignment enables the students to display creativity, to improve interpersonal skills, as well as to develop presentation and communication abilities. The presentation could be presented in the usual in-class format or in a more innovative style using a videotaped presentation. An example of the videotape presentation assignment is described below.

Teams of 6 to 8 students will be assigned to present an 8 to 10 minute dramatic interpretation based on the book *The Bottom Line is Betrayal*. The presentation may portray actual situations and characters directly from the novel, or the presentation may feature settings and characters invented by the students but based on concepts described in the novel. Each group will be required to submit a typed report and videotape of their presentation. Your typed report should include the following: 1) the title of the presentation; 2) the group number and names of group members; 3) a "screen play" of the presentation which includes all the dialogue as well as props that will be used; 4) the goals of the presentation (e.g. auditing a company, handling personnel or ethical problems, launching a new product, expanding into an international market, etc.); and 5) how these goals were achieved by the presentation.

The key to effectively completing this assignment is proper planning. Before the group begins filming, the script should be prepared and rehearsed. Any necessary props should be obtained and on-hand. Each member of the team should conscientiously fulfill his or her part of the assignment. When filming, be sure to include the title of the presentation and names of the group members at the beginning of the film (you can write this information on paper and film it for 8 or 10 seconds).

Prior to submission of the report and tape, an outline of the presentation must be submitted. The date the outline is due is shown on your syllabus. The outline should follow the same format as the report, except the screen play does not have to be in a word-for-word format but only in an outline format. The report and tape will be graded by your instructor. Also, the class will view and evaluate the tape. Both report and tape will be evaluated for educational value, originality, creativity, drama/humor, and technical merit (can you hear it, can you see it). The presentation should stimulate interest in the subject matter through a more entertaining format than a simple lecture.

INDEX

INDEX

INDEX

INDEX

INDEX

ABOUT THE AUTHOR

Katherine Taken Smith was born in Chicago, Illinois, USA. She received her baccalaureate degree from Northeast Louisiana University, her masters and doctorate from Louisiana Tech University. She serves on the editorial boards of several professional journals and has presented her work at business conferences in the U.S. and abroad. She resides in College Station, Texas with her husband and three children. For more information about the author and **The Bottom Line is Betrayal**, check the Web site: http://www.IOL19.com/murphy/novels/novels.htm